John Glassco

Selected Poems
with
Three Notes on the Poetic Process

Acknowledgements

I am grateful to William Toye for his help and advice. The Glassco material in this volume is published with his kind permission as Literary Executor for the Estate of John Glassco.

I would also like to thank for their assistance and cooperation, the National Library of Canada, the Rare Book Room, McLennan Library, McGill University, the Beinecke Rare Book and Manuscript Library, Yale University, all of which house segments of John Glassco's papers and letters, as well as Oxford University Press (Canada), the original publishers of the *Selected Poems*. Dr. Duff Hicks kindly briefed me on the ravages of Buerger's disease.

The following NOTE appeared in the original edition

Many of these poems were taken from *The Deficit Made Flesh* (1958) and *A Point of Sky* (1964). Others have appeared more recently in *Alphabet, Delta, Poetry* (Chicago), *Queen's Quarterly, Saturday Night* and *Yes*.

I wish to express my thanks to A.J.M. Smith for his invaluable help in choosing and arranging them.

J.G.

John Glassco

Selected Poems
with
Three Notes on the Poetic Process

arranged
with Introduction and Notes
by
Michael Gnarowski

The Golden Dog Press
Ottawa – Canada – 1997

Canadian Cataloguing in Publication Data

Glassco, John, 1909–1981
    Selected poems : with three notes on the poetic process

ISBN 0-919614-62-0

I. Gnarowski, Michael, 1934–   II. Title.

| PS8513.L388S44 1997 | C811'.54 | C96-900405-2 |
| PR9199.3.G574S44 1997 | | |

Printed in Canada

Cover design: The Gordon Creative Group of Ottawa.

Typesetting and layout: Carleton Production Centre, Nepean.

Distributed by:
    PROLOGUE INC.
    1650 Lionel-Bertrand Boulevard,
    Boisbriand, Québec, Canada, J7H 1N7
    Tel: (514) 434-0306 / 1-800-363-2864
    Fax: (514) 434-2627 / 1-800-361-8088

The Golden Dog Press wishes to express its appreciation to the Canada Council and the Ontario Arts Council for current and past support of its publishing programme.

Table of Contents

Illustrations

Remembering Buffy, who once inscribed these words:

haec otiosa sedulitas ...

To Mike
Gnarowski,
with
affection
[signature]
23.6.64

John Glassco in a "studio-type" photograph of the mid-sixties

John Glassco
An Introduction, Chiefly Biographical

Of John Glassco (1909–1981), it may reasonably be said that although he lived to be seventy one, his writing life, or at least that part of it which came to public notice, spanned a relatively short period of some fifteen years. To those who knew him he professed himself to be a failure, and spent a great deal of time in the grip of indecision, tormented by what he perceived to be the inadequacy of what he had written. Later in life he claimed to have destroyed much of his early work, so that any attempt at following his development is necessarily dependent on what evidence can be gleaned from fugitive pieces and odd references preserved, here and there, in his journals, correspondence and private conversations.

Although there is a clear sense of an orderly spirit witnessed in such of his papers as now survive in public depositories, there is, nevertheless, no escaping an awareness that interesting materials have vanished, and that these *lacunæ* are the cross that those inquiring into Glassco's life must bear.

He was born on December the 15th, in 1909, into the middle ranks of the anglophile establishment of early twentieth-century Montreal, and was destined for the kind of comfortable life and eventual career in the church or the professions that privileged status bestowed on the scions and the less ambitious offspring of Montreal's anglophone élite. Glassco's family was very well-to-do on his mother's side, his grandfather having founded a successful financial institution, the Guarantee Company of North America, which had made him a prominent member of Montreal's, and therefore, in those halcyon days for that city, of Canada's financial community. Glassco's father, a trained engineer, was Secretary and Bursar of McGill University, and, in the administrative hierarchy of that great institution, stood second only to the Principal, Sir Arthur Currie, G.C.M.G., K.C.B., LL.D., one of Canada's distinguished generals of the First World War.

But while all of this should have ensured an easy life and a smooth passage into the ranks of Canada's élite for the young Glassco, what we find in reality is an unhappy adolescent scarred by paternal abuse

1

and determined to escape the role for which he was being fashioned, first by private schooling[1] and, ultimately, by the prospect of career-related studies that were to be undertaken at McGill University. Bowing unhappily to his parents' wishes, Glassco entered McGill as a fifteen-year-old freshman, and proceeded to spend, according to his own account, three seemingly uninteresting years at the university, all the while plotting his escape from a hated family environment and the stifling constraints of a provincial city.

At McGill Glassco met Graeme Taylor, a slightly older and unusually cynical individual who was to become a negative but important presence in the first half of Glassco's mature life. He also came into brief and glancing contact with a group of students led by Arthur Smith, Frank Scott and Leon Edel, which was engaged in infusing the spirit of a newly discovered modernism into the pages of *The McGill Daily Literary Supplement*, destined to become a bolder vehicle of the modernist line as *The McGill Fortnightly Review*.[2] Quarrelling with his father and seeking a way out of his unhappiness, Glassco left home shortly after the beginning of the fall term in 1927. He struggled on at university supporting himself by odd jobs, but some time in January or February of 1928 he dropped out and went to work as a clerk at the Sun Life Assurance Company, where Graeme Taylor was already employed in a similar capacity. As he relates it in the fictionalized autobiography of his youth, *Memoirs of Montparnasse* (1970, 1995), Glassco and his companion Graeme Taylor had set their sights on Paris, an adventure upon which they embarked early in 1928. It is worth noting that Glassco claimed to have travelled to England as early as the summer of 1926, and that he visited Paris then, falling in love with the city and vowing to return. The second voyage, though, was meant to be a more serious and permanent commitment to a city that promised freedom of lifestyle and,

---

[1] Glassco was enrolled in Selwyn House School, from which he graduated in 1923; he was then sent to Bishop's College School in Lennoxville, Quebec, and, finally for a six-month stint, to Lower Canada College. [Source: "Autobiographical Sketch" dated June 9th, 1961.]

[2] To quote his own words: "I did little or nothing at McGill for three years, barely getting through my examinations, but doing an enormous amount of reading on my own. I moved on the edge of literary and intellectual circles in McGill, published a few minor pieces in *The McGill Fortnightly Review*, and conducted a satirical column in *The McGill Daily* called 'The Goosestep'. More importantly, I met Graeme Taylor ... " ["Autobiographical Sketch".]

presumably, offered the opportunity for creative inspiration. However, the sojourn in Paris was not one marked by great industry or productivity on Glassco's or Taylor's part. The *Memoirs* offers ample evidence that the two would-be writers threw themselves with greater dedication into meeting people and having a good time, than into realising their creative ambitions.[3] Although Glassco claims to have written poetry while in Paris, and even to have experimented with surrealism, no tangible evidence of this writing appears to have survived from this period other than Glassco's own and oft-repeated assertion in the form of bio-bibliographical listings of what may very well have been phantom publications.[4]

In spite of the happy-go-lucky circumstances that characterised the Paris experience, we know that this episode in Glassco's life ended in a near tragedy. He returned to Canada emotionally depleted and suffering from a serious infection that required major, risk-laden surgery, resulting in the removal of one lung. It is with

---

[3]That Glassco and Taylor, "tutored" in their Paris life by the hard-drinking Robert McAlmon (1896–1956), projected the image of a determined dilettantism may be deduced from a snide item that appeared on page 354 in *This Quarter* (Vol. III, No. 2), then under the editorship of Edward W. Titus, the wealthy publisher of The Black Manikin Press and disaffected husband of Helena Rubinstein, the queen of the cosmetics industry. The item in question, bearing the caption "Bistro Highbrows", must have had Glassco and his bosom pals in mind. It reads, in part,

> Two young aspirants to literary spurs, snug under the frayed wings of a much older aspirant, stumbled upon the discovery of the truth known at least since the days of Johann Gensfleisch Gutenberg that a higgledy-piggledy throwing together of words alone is not sufficient to produce literature; that literature must have substance or "content". In other words, like nature, it abhors a vacuum. This they proceeded to tell the world, via numerous Montparnasse bistros.

[4]A poem entitled *Conan's Fig*, and ostensibly published as a pamphlet by the avant-garde periodical *transition* (1927–1938) in 1928, is claimed by Glassco to be a product of his stay in Paris. A sonnet-like snippet of it is supposed to have survived as lines fifty-seven to seventy of the poem, "The Day", in *A Point of Sky*.

That *Conan's Fig* must have existed in some form or other is attested to in a Journal entry of July 30th, 1936 in which Glassco, ruminating on his poetic life, says, "What a lot of nonsense I did write in those days!" In the margin he has written "*Conan's Fig*. What tripe!"

One of the illustrations in the present volume is a list of publications, initialled by Glassco, that he had compiled and submitted to the periodical *Yes* (1956–1969), which was preparing a special issue on his work. *Conan's Fig* is first on the list, and it also appears as the first item under the "By the Same Author" heading in Glassco's *Selected Poems*.

JOHN GLASSCO: LIST OF PUBLICATIONS IN BOOK FORM

VERSE

*Conan's Fig. (Pamphlet). Paris, transition, 1928.

*(French translation by Robert Desnos, Figue de Conan, Paris, Kra, 1930).

The Deficit Made Flesh. Toronto, McClelland & Stewart, 1958.

A Point of Sky. Toronto, Oxford University Press, 1964.

FICTION

*Contes en crinoline. (In French). Paris, Gaucher, 1930.

*(Anon. German translation, Märchen in Krinoline, Leipzig, 1931).

Under the Hill. Completion of unfinished novel by Aubrey Beardsley, with critical introduction. Illus. Paris, Olympia Press, 1959.

TRANSLATION

The Journal of Saint-Denys-Garneau. Toronto, McClelland & Stewart, 1962.

PSEUDONYMOUS NOVEL

The English Governess, by Miles Underwood. Paris, Olympia Press, 1960. (Banned in England and U. S. A. Publisher prosecuted by French Govt., 1962; remaining stock seized, 1963, and now held in France).

Feb. 27, 1964

JOHN GLASSCO.
FOSTER, QUE.
CANADA

*I haven't even got copies of these myself. J.G.

List of publications submitted by Glassco to the editors of *Yes* for their September 1966 issue featuring his work.

this event, and the attendant prolonged stay in hospital, that we enter upon the nineteen thirties, a period of convalescence, artistic vacillation and considerable self-doubt for Glassco.

Recovered — somewhat — from his operation, and the beneficiary of an inheritance from his grandfather's estate, Glassco found the nineteen thirties, nevertheless, to be not without promise or possibility. Graeme Taylor and he rented a series of houses in and around Montreal, eventually finding their way to the Eastern Townships of Quebec where Glassco chose, ultimately, to put down his roots,[5] and where he remained in fairly permanent residence until his death. The best source that we have for an account of this period is his own journal, which is marked by hypochondria and the self-doubt so characteristic of Glassco's personality. The entry for March 28th, 1934[6] is typical of this state of mind and is worth quoting:

> I am beginning to believe that I may not just have it in me to write poetry.

and a little later:

> My only consolation is that Graeme is a really good poet and him I almost regard as part of myself. This winter I have certainly not been productive. I have not <u>finished</u> one single poem.

However, we also witness his struggle to find a voice, and are struck by the prevalence of references to contemporary writers who could only have been described as traditionalist, and the frequent hieing back, in mind, spirit and craft, to the masters of the preceding century(ies). Suffused with a kind of literary anglophilia, he seemed unable to enter boldly into the modernist experiment of the twentieth century, as he cast admiring glances at the likes of Edith Sitwell, Rupert Brooke and Robert Graves; took into his favour Robert Bridges, Edmund Blunden, Siegfried Sassoon, Roy Campbell and Gerard Manley Hopkins (he tries to write a sonnet in sprung rhythm), and saw himself as a minor version of A.E. Housman whom he claimed to have met in Paris. His ambition, he notes, is to create a book of poems on "simple and perhaps sentimental themes", not unlike those

---

[5]Using part of his inheritance, Glassco bought a property known as "The Jones Farm" in 1936. It became the inspiration for the poem "The White Mansion".

[6]Glassco Papers. Rare Book Room, McLennan Library, McGill University, Montreal, Quebec.

expressed in *A Shropshire Lad*. He semed to be wrapped up in that
sentiment so prevalent in much of English poetry between the Wars
and described by Cyril Connolly, that perceptive chronicler of En-
glish letters during that period, as "romanticism in decay, shielded
from its logical consequences by good mixing, Anglican ethics, Victo-
rianism." When Graeme Taylor[7] completes a story called "The Vol-
unteer", Glassco can only think of *Blackwood's* as the logical venue
for it, and when, early in 1936, he finds that he can cobble together
a sheaf of some ten poems, he wants to send them to *The London
Mercury*. Even T.S. Eliot is found wanting and is dismissed with:

> I have at last cast off T.S. Eliot. After reading his 'Selected Es-
> says' last night I see what he is — merely a professional soul of
> great ingenuity for whom life seems to consist of a handful of
> quotations.   (Journal, McGill University, February 1st, 1936)

A traditionalist to the core, Glassco, again in Connolly's words, was
a perfect example of the kind of individual who saw literature as a
"fanciful pastime of well-to-do middle-aged children who had re-
fused to grow up". As a result, he fretted away the decade of the
thirties worrying about blank verse, the sonnet form, and the num-
ber of lines of verse that he had managed to write. The dilettante
found expression in Journal entries such as the following penned on
July 15th, 1934:

> I think I would give up writing if I had anything else to do.

It is clear that he was wounded in body and spirit, and overshad-
owed by the presence of Graeme Taylor. The Journal is full of the
sense of his worthlessness and of his directionless floundering, yet he
continued to struggle, trying to write and recording many instances
of starts and stutters of what became later aborted or disavowed
projects. To complicate matters, there is evidence that Glassco was
troubled by the ambiguities of his own sexuality. His relationship
with Taylor is not a clear-cut case of an exclusively homosexual union.
In the late summer of 1935, in August of that year, he embarks on a
prolonged ritual of the seduction of Adrienne, a young woman who

---

[7]Graeme Taylor was not without literary ambition. When in Paris he showed more
diligence in the pursuit of the writer's craft and managed to get slightly more material
(fiction) into print than Glassco.

happens to be staying at a neighbour's house. It is clear that Graeme is aware of this design on someone whom Glassco describes as "the virgin mistress" and who succumbs, more or less, to Glassco's advances. Three years later, the enigmatic figure of 'Sappho' arrives at the country house in the Townships. With her there springs up a *ménage à trois*, which serves to scandalise the locals and, four years later almost to the day, sees Sappho and Graeme Taylor married. These were war years and Taylor had enlisted in the Hussars in October of 1941. Shortly after Taylor's marriage to Sappho, a distraught Glassco notes in his Journal:

> Graeme married to Sappho, my worst fear living here on the farm without him ... " [August 11th, 1941]

A month later Glassco applies to join the Air Force but is turned down, and is thus diverted to less spectacular wartime activity: the delivery of the rural mail, an experience from which will begin to flow the reflective poems so characteristic of his new-found voice. This is a development attended by a new kind of confidence, as Glassco begins to publish poems in the *Canadian Forum* and prose excerpts in *First Statement*. The output is modest at first, with the ripple of submissions going out as far as *The Fiddlehead* in Fredericton. All of this is taking place in the last two years of the war and the period immediately following. Later, in the latter half of the nineteen fifties, there will be poems in *Yes* and *Delta*, and a more determined reaching out to the literary community, of which Glassco had always been such a diffident member. Undoubtedly the major event of these years for Glassco was the death of Graeme Taylor[8] who was diagnosed, in November of 1956, with an illness that Glassco described

---

[8]The significance of Graeme Taylor's death for Glassco's growth as a writer is clearly conveyed in this observation that Glassco recorded in his Journal. Distractedly, Glassco gets the year wrong and enters '1956' rather than '1957' as the year of Taylor's death. He wrote:

> As for life, Graeme died in February 1956 [sic]. It seems much longer ago than that — I suppose because since then life has been unbelievably richer, fuller, freer. Here, if nowhere else, can I admit that this was a blessed thing for me (for him too, perhaps, though how should I know?), and should have happened ten years before it did. I have never realised before how great a clog & a drag he was on me, with that everlasting discouragement, depression, cynicism & passionate insistence on no effort or idea being worthwhile. Indeed it sometimes terrifies me to think how almost entirely so much of my life was wasted on him & how very

Continued from front flap

During the twenties and thirties John Glassco contributed stories and occasional pieces to the *McGill Fortnightly Review* and the *avant-garde* Parisian magazines, *transition* and *This Quarter,* but it was not until more recently when some of his country poems were published in the *Canadian Forum* that Mr. Glassco began to attract the attention he deserves. These poems are an authentic expression of his interest in rural life and the raising of horses. He has bred hackney ponies from his stallion, Royal Satin, and in 1951 founded the Foster Horse Show, now recognized as one of the leading events in the Eastern Townships. Many of his best pieces were composed while driving a rural mail route during the war. "Driving a horse on country roads," he says, "is favourable to poetic composition. You can lay the reins down and look around you."

Besides his eclogues and bucolic verses, Mr. Glassco has written poems of a personal and psychological nature which testify to the wide range of his experience and the catholicity of his literary taste. He fuses a modern and a classical spirit in a way that is peculiarly his own, and this thoroughly mature volume makes a new and extremely valuable contribution to contemporary Canadian poetry.

A. J. M. SMITH

INDIAN FILE

Out of the tremendous volume of verse that is written year by year in Canada it is possible to choose the work of only a very few poets for separate publication. In our Indian File books we have attempted to bring out as a series the best new work of some of these contemporary Canadian poets. It has been the consistent aim of our editors to select writers of marked creative ability and to reject any work that does not conform to a high standard of originality and technical competence. We believe that they have compiled a series of which Canadians can be proud.

In keeping with the distinctive quality of the poetry in the Indian File series we have used covers designed by Paul Arthur which are based on the decorative designs of the West Coast and Plains Indians.

1: DEEPER INTO THE FOREST by Roy Daniells

2: THE STRENGTH OF THE HILLS by Robert Finch

3: THE RED HEART by James Reaney (Out of Print) [Governor-General's Award]

4: OF TIME AND THE LOVER by James Wreford [Governor-General's Award]

5: BORDER RIVER by Alfred Goldsworthy Bailey

6: THE COLOUR AS NAKED by Patrick Anderson

7: THE METAL AND THE FLOWER by P. K. Page [Governor-General's Award]

8: EVEN YOUR RIGHT EYE by Phyllis Webb

9: THE DEFICIT MADE FLESH by John Glassco

McCLELLAND AND STEWART LIMITED
Publishers   Toronto

Dust jacket of *The Deficit Made Flesh* (1958) with the two inside flaps carrying A.J.M. Smith's endorsement *cum* blurb.

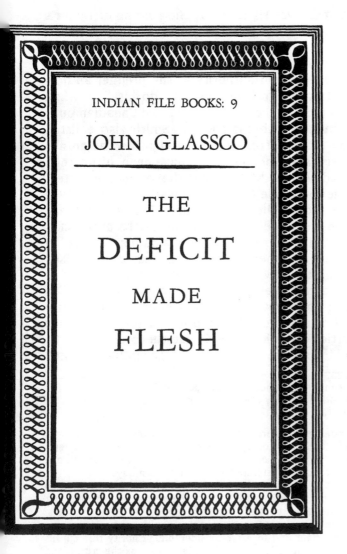

INDIAN FILE BOOKS: 9

JOHN GLASSCO

THE

DEFICIT

MADE

FLESH

THE DEFICIT MADE FLESH

By John Glassco

The poems of John Glassco are something new in Canadian poetry, but there is nothing hasty or ill-digested about them. They are the products of a mature sensibility, and they assimilate disparate and even discordant elements of experience. This subject matter is rural life in the Eastern Townships of Quebec. Understanding and sympathy are deepened by the poet's complex and genuinely sophisticated viewpoint, which combines an aesthetic with a genuinely moral code of values. The little pocket of country isolation—a country of the mind as well as a fading, arduous, and dedicated way of life—is presented as a kind of forlorn and heroic rejection of the evils of mechanization and success-worship of the acquisitive society. In such descriptive pieces as "The Entailed Farm," "The Rural Mail," "Stud Groom," and "Deserted Buildings under Shefford Mountain," the spirit of John Clare or Edward Thomas seems to have been introduced into Canadian verse. Actually a modern consciousness that shares something of the allusive richness of Proust's has here found its most natural expression in a classical poetry that is at once local and universal.

Continued on back flap

as Buerger's disease,[9] and to which he succumbed in February of 1957.

The new beginning that was signalled by the passing of Taylor's influence from Glassco's life was marked by the assembling of a small sheaf of poems with which Glassco approached A.J.M. Smith, a sometime acquaintance from the days of the 1920's at McGill and now at the height of his influence and authority as the premier anthologist of Canadian poetry.[10] Smith promised to do his best while warning Glassco not to raise his hopes too high since Canadian publishers were "timid, money-grubbing souls". Smith also enlisted the Toronto poet, Jay Macpherson, whom he identified as an admirer of Glassco's poetry, and who appears to have been, ultimately, responsible for persuading Jack McClelland, the young and enterprising publisher/owner of McClelland and Stewart Limited, to take the manuscript for his Indian File Books, where *The Deficit Made Flesh* appeared in 1958 as number nine in the Series. Its dust jacket carried an endorsement-like blurb on its two inside flaps signed by Smith which, besides mis-statements concerning Glassco's supposed involvement with modernist activity in Paris and at McGill, helped to foster the idea that Glassco's poetry was "rural" and "bucolic". This refrain would be taken up by reviewers, and would echo in Munro Beattie's appraisal of Glassco for the *Literary History of Canada* (1965), although Beattie was quick to recognise the latent sophistication of the poet and the stylist. The collection, generally speaking,

---

       nearly the rest of it might have been wasted too, but for the accident
       of his death, Good God, how lucky I was! [Journal, McGill University,
       September 16th, 1960]

[9]A painful illness, commonly encountered as a disease in younger (20–40) men who smoke, and characterised by a blockage of the arteries, occurring usually in the legs. Glassco mentions in his Journal that Taylor is facing the prospect of a wheelchair, and then goes on to say that his companion suffered terribly in his last days.

[10]A.J.M. Smith (1902–1980) was a product of McGill University where, while still an undergraduate, he was instrumental in organising a circle of young modernists that included the poets F.R. Scott (1899–1985) and Leo Kennedy (b. 1907) among others, and who helped to promote modernism in Canadian writing. Smith went on to become a significant poet in his own right and to exert considerable authority through his efforts as an anthologist. His major and most influential work was the critical and historical anthology, *The Book of Canadian Poetry* (1943, 1948, 1957), which became a standard teaching tool for schools and universities alike. Glassco, incidentally, did not make it into any one of the three editions of this seminal collection, and had to wait for inclusion until Smith edited *The Oxford Book of Canadian Verse* (1960).

produced a number of gratifying responses. The reviews were mixed but not unfriendly, while at the same time, there was the balm of a fawning letter from Al Purdy, who thought that at least two of the poems in the collection were "masterpieces", and a letter from Ralph Gustafson, the compiler of the not insignificant *Penguin Book of Canadian Verse*, who expressed his regret at not having been aware of Glassco's material when assembling his own anthology.[11]

At about the same time, Glassco had been made aware of the possibilities of translation, a challenge to which he was led by F.R. Scott, who was himself involved in translating French-Canadian poetry. This activity would become a major preoccupation for Glassco, whose sensitivity and success as a translator would win him accolades, and result in the creation of a translators' prize named after him. His achievement, though, was in the fine work he did in translating *The Journal of Saint-Denys-Garneau* (1962) and the *Complete Poems of Saint Denys Garneau* (1975), and in compiling and translating many of the poems in his *The Poetry of French Canada in Translation* (1970). In general, it is the decade of the 1960's that represents and envelops Glassco's best years. Properly launched with his first collection of poems, and actively submitting to the buoyant little magazine scene of the time, he was quickly taken up by the literary establishment. He found his way into the glossier literary periodicals as well, publishing in *The Tamarack Review*, *Saturday Night* and, internationally, in *Poetry Australia* and *Adam International Review*. His friendship with Smith and Scott also paid its dividends. They were not only happy to write letters on his behalf to the Canada Council in support of Glassco's applications but, as Oxford University Press authors themselves, helped to bring him into that prestigious fold.

That the sixties were an enormously important and productive period for Glassco becomes evident when we consider the range and volume of his output. No small credit for this is due to his having

---

[11]Ralph Gustafson (1909–1995), then resident in New York, had compiled the widely-distributed *Anthology of Canadian Poetry (English)*, which came out under the Pelican Books imprint in 1942 and, reportedly, was one of a number of books made available as reading matter to Allied troops during the war. It later became *The Penguin Book of Canadian Verse* (1958) and was reissued, revised and enlarged, in 1967. Three of Glassco's poems were included in the latter edition, by a Gustafson who had returned to Canada and was living in North Hatley in the Eastern Townships where he was very much part of the community of poets that included A.J.M. Smith, F.R. Scott, John Glassco and D.G. Jones.

shed, successfully, the negative effects of his earlier life with Graeme
Taylor. Not only was his creativity transformed from a state marked
by the occasional poem to one of an active pursuit of projects and
ideas on several fronts, but his life, too, underwent a profound
change. He had met Elma von Colmar in 1956, and their attachment
would lead to marriage after the death of Taylor. It was a union
that rekindled Glassco's spirit and prompted him to see clearly the
possibilities that a writing life would offer to him. He returned to
Paris in 1958, seeking renewal and rediscovery, and even attempted
to establish permanent residence there the following year. Although
the decade opened with the shadow of illness and a prolonged stay
in hospital for Glassco,[12] he was, nevertheless, on an upward curve
that would draw him out of his previously reclusive existence into the
limelight of the heady years of the Centennial decade. While in hos-
pital, Glassco completed work on the manuscript of his translation of
The Journal of Saint-Denys-Garneau and began to move ahead with
plans to return, yet one more time, to Paris. These visits to Paris, in
the company of his wife Elma, were in themselves a tonic that helped
to recapture some of the spirit and uplift of the Paris of his youth.
They, together with a resurgence of interest in the Paris of the 1920's,
marked by the publication of the memoirs and reminiscences of such
notables of the time such as Sylvia Beach, Callaghan and Heming-
way, prompted Glassco to think in terms of his own "remembrance
of things past". With his memories alive once more, he began work
on what would become, some seven years later, his own *Memoirs
of Montparnasse*. But that was not all. Supported by the social
skills of his wife, and now fully integrated into the circle of writers
that was centred on the Eastern Townships, Glassco assumed, what
was for him, the uncharacteristic role of *animateur* as well as that
of literary activist. First he organised the Foster Poetry Conference
on English poetry in Quebec,[13] which was held in October of 1963.
On the heels of that event, he was chosen to organise and host, on

---

[12] Glassco became ill in the autumn of 1960 with a lingering cold that developed into
tuberculosis and required an extended stay in hospital. He spent most of 1961 at the
Royal Edward Laurentian Hospital in Ste. Agathe, north of Montreal. He wrote about
this experience in "A Season in Limbo", and saw it published under the pseudonym
of Silas N. Gooch in *The Tamarack Review* (#23, Spring 1962).

[13] The Conference was held in Foster, where he was living, and the papers read were
published as *English Poetry in Quebec: Proceedings of the Foster Poetry Conference
October 12–14, 1963* (Montreal: McGill University Press, 1965).

behalf of the Canada Council, a gathering of poets at Stanley House, the former Vice-Regal fishing lodge on the Baie des Chaleurs in the Gaspé, which took place in July of 1964. In the same year the Oxford University Press published *A Point of Sky*, a collection of his poems that, in terms of poetic output, was only fourteen pages ampler than *The Deficit* volume of eight years earlier. From the early 1960's Glassco had begun to appear with some regularity in the pages of *The Tamarack Review*, and it was also at about this time that he was approached by the editors of *Yes*, a Montreal-based literary periodical, for a representative sampling of his writing intended as a centrepiece item in a forthcoming issue of the magazine.[14]

Glassco had been developing his skills, as well, since the late 1950's, in a genre in which he took some quiet pride while remaining reticent about the depth of his interest or the true scope of its nature. Its beginnings lie with Glassco's long-standing interest in what has been aptly termed the "literature of detumescence". There is occasional mention of erotica in his Journal, and from time to time he records the arrival (despite the vigilant efforts of the customs service) of one item or another of titillating literature. But a real involvement with the world of pornography begins when Glassco connects with Maurice Girodias, the unjustly infamous publisher of the Olympia Press of Paris with whom Glassco first places his skilfully completed text of Aubrey Beardsley's[15] unfinished work, *The Story of Venus and Tannhäuser*. Not only did Girodias publish Glassco's text entitled *Under the Hill* in 1959 in a handsome, casebound edition, but he also made it number 105 in his predominantly pornographic Traveller's

---

[14]Glassco had established contact with the people editing *Yes* as early as 1957, and had been submitting poetry, off and on, to that little magazine since that time. The prospect of a "feature" issue was an interesting development in Glassco's career because it would offer a cross-section of his writing thereby providing a sense of his varied interests. He submitted poetry, maxims and reflections (enjoying the borrowing and the "joke" on La Rochefoucauld enormously), translations and even an excerpt from the as yet unpublished *Temple of Pederasty*. The "John Glassco" issue of *Yes 15* appeared in September of 1966.

[15]Aubrey Vincent Beardsley (1872–1898), English illustrator and writer known for his decadent and erotic art. He was one of the group that challenged society with its *fin-de-siècle* sensuality, and was touched by the scandal that destroyed Oscar Wilde (1854–1900). Beardsley's erotic novel, *The Story of Venus and Tannhäuser*, was originally published in a censored text as *Under the Hill* in *The Yellow Book* (1894–1897), a journal considered shocking for its time. An unexpurgated version was privately issued in 1907.

Cover of *Yes 15* with its "A John Glassco Issue" banner.

"La chaleur du brandon Vénus."
— *LE ROMAN DE LA ROSE*

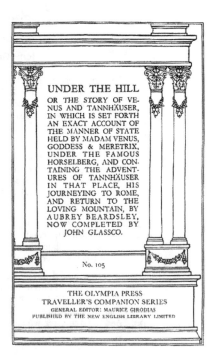

UNDER THE HILL
OR *THE* STORY OF VE-
NUS AND TANNHÄUSER,
IN WHICH IS SET FORTH
AN EXACT ACCOUNT OF
THE MANNER OF STATE
HELD BY MADAM VENUS,
GODDESS & MERETRIX,
UNDER THE FAMOUS
HORSELBERG, AND CON-
TAINING THE ADVENT-
URES OF TANNHÄUSER
IN THAT PLACE, HIS
JOURNEYING TO ROME,
AND RETURN TO THE
LOVING MOUNTAIN, BY
AUBREY BEARDSLEY,
NOW COMPLETED BY
JOHN GLASSCO.

No. 105

THE OLYMPIA PRESS
TRAVELLER'S COMPANION SERIES
GENERAL EDITOR: MAURICE GIRODIAS
PUBLISHED BY THE NEW ENGLISH LIBRARY LIMITED

Frontispiece and titlepage of *Under the Hill* (1959, 1966) in the Traveller's
Companion Series. The design was an adaptation of the one (unused) that
Aubrey Beardsley had devised for *Venus and Tannhäuser* in 1895.

The Needham Cemetery

by

JOHN GLASSCO

"A sightly place," says Luke Orlando Ball
In *The History of Brome County*, "sandy of soil,
Easy of access, level and well drained.
You never saw the Dead so well maintained."
— Never, indeed: here corpses seldom spoil

Even in the wettest year—and this meant much
To folk who raise their eyes to heaven but keep
Their feet upon the dear familiar ground
Which wore them out, as they went round and round
And to and fro: a kind of thinking sheep.

Being slow to grasp, they liked the second look,
And short of sight, they favoured the long view;
But all that happened was that, right or wrong,
One came too late, the other took too long:
Time led them here, as it was bound to do.

As it was bound to do. And still the dead
Lecture their children on the way to live.
The blood's didactic can perpetuate
The useless virtues which are out of date,
And antique vices which we half forgive

Draw close, lean down, let the communal voice
Of a dead shrouded elder testify
Out of the soil he thought of first and last—
Even in his hours of leisure, which he passed
In waiting for his enemies to die—:

"Mind your own business. Owe no man a cent.
Keep out of trouble and away from war.
Don't trust a Frenchman. Be nobody's fool:
Nothing for nothing is the golden rule;
God lives in walls, the devil keeps the door.

Off-print from *Queen's Quarterly* Vol. 72, No. 3 (Autumn 1965) of "The Needham Cemetery".

THE NEEDHAM CEMETERY

"Look to the end. Pride goes before a fall.
The one mistake, remember, is to grow
Too big for your breeches: that's where Agag dulled
And how the tipsy Amalekites were fooled:
And Jezebel flew high but landed low.

"All flesh is grass: so keep the meadows up,
The hired man down, the women in their place;
Let your whole life turn with the turning year,
Obedient to the seasons. Have no fear
Lest hardness hood your eyes or twist your face,

For sweet goes bad, but sour goes on forever. . .
So look at your feet, your fields, the things you own,
And find man's meaning there: cows in the barn,
Crop in the mow and taxes paid. The farm,
The farm is the whole of life—what death alone

"Can take from you, giving himself instead
In whom its guardian and its genius move.
So interwoven is the daily round
(Dust in the air and silence underground)
That out of him you make your second love. . ."

These counsels of perfection I have heard
In the autumn wind that sighs above these stones
Covered with angels, roses, pointing hands,
Witnessing what life gives and death demands
On a dry hillside full of farmers' bones.

Companion Series in which Glassco joined the illustrious company
of Henry Miller, Samuel Beckett, Jean Cocteau, William Burroughs
and Vladimir Nabokov, to name a few of the best-known and most
serious writers in that notorious stable. In 1960 Girodias brought
out Glassco's flagellationist fantasy, *The English Governess*,[16] under
the pseudonymous "cover" of Miles Underwood. In a way, this and
several other works[17] of like kind served as a special preoccupation
for Glassco and gave his sexual interests a legitimate literary outlet.

But — and his skill as a translator notwithstanding — it is as a poet
and as an engagingly prevaricating memoirist that Glassco has a firm
claim on his standing as a writer of considerable accomplishment.
When he published *A Point of Sky* in 1964, he showed that he had
found his voice, and although the register would be a narrow one, it
is nevertheless true that what he offered his readers was carefully fin-
ished work which bore the high gloss of much revising. An example
of this polishing — even after publication — is seen in the emended
off-print of "The Needham Cemetery", which appeared in *Queen's
Quarterly* in 1965 and is reproduced here. It underwent some al-
teration in 1966, and was further improved, if only slightly, for its
inclusion in *Selected Poems* (1970). In a different kind of significant
"tinkering" or transformation, "Ode: The Autumn Resurrection",
a poem given pride of place in that it opens *A Point of Sky*, had
its beginnings as a composition called "Summer", and, in a much
more important incarnation, existed as a Wordsworthian echo in its
manuscript version when it was named "The Invitations". Similarly
a poem originally conceived as something called "Emotions" led to

---

[16] The publishing history of this work is curious, to say the least. It exists in a "dirty"
version supposedly written at the behest of Girodias and published in Paris in 1960. It
was then followed by later "dirty" and "clean" versions, some translated and some pi-
rated, with variations in the title and all appearing anonymously or pseudonymously.
The Canadian edition, published as *Harriet Marwood, Governess* (1976), is the only
one to bear Glassco's name.

[17] These works, at least two of which are heavily indebted to their original authors,
included *The Temple of Pederasty* (1970), which had appeared in 1928 as *Quaint Sto-
ries of Samurais* with its titlepage giving Saikaku Ibara as the author and Ken Sato (see
note 19) as the putative translator "from the old original"; *The Fatal Woman* (1974),
an assemblage of three erotic tales; and *Venus in Furs* (1977), in what is very likely
a "cribbed" text purportedly translated by Glassco from the German of its author,
Leopold von Sacher-Masoch (1835–1895), an Austrian novelist whose interest in sex-
ual pleasure derived from subjection and physical pain, gave the term "masochism"
to the language.

"Deserted Buildings under Shefford Mountain", referred to by the poet as "my best poem".[18]

While it is true that Glassco did not have a great many new poems to show for the eight years between the appearance of *The Deficit Made Flesh* and that of *A Point of Sky,* he had been busy in that time at his translating, his erotica and his organising of conferences. He was also in the throes of writing fiction, submitting it to publishers, of suffering the crushing disappointment of having it returned, and of re-writing his reminiscence of his stay in Paris. From the middle of the 1960's three important lines of creative thrust for Glassco pointed towards, and converged upon, 1970–1971, a span of a little more than a year, which was to be the *apogée* of his writing life. It would see the publication of his *Memoirs of Montparnasse*, of *The Poetry of French Canada in Translation*, and of his *Selected Poems*. For the latter, Glassco would win the Governor General's Award in 1971. The publication of three major books within such a short period was in itself a remarkable achievement, and what was significant as a symbol of his status in the writing community as well, was that all three appeared under the imprint of Oxford University Press.

The decade of the seventies, then, had begun auspiciously enough, but in spite of the reassurance of his achievements, Glassco's powers had begun to wane. Certainly, the vein of his own originality had begun to run out. With the exception of the publication in booklet form of his twenty-three-page poem *Montreal* in 1973, and the gathering and publication in 1974, under the title *The Fatal Woman*, of three novellas that had been lying around in his desk drawer for a long time, Glassco had obviously shifted into translation and adaptation as a likely outlet for his creative energies. Moreover, he had lost his wife Elma late in 1971, and although a happy second marriage to Marion McCormick, herself an accomplished writer and media journalist, brought him new friends and new interests, Glassco was clearly headed for the literary sidelines. To be sure, there was still a quite impressive output of writing in what would prove to be the last phase of his life. He published a few poems in leading journals, gave interviews on the radio and appeared at literary functions. In 1970 he had published *The Temple of Pederasty*[19] with a quirky California

---

[18] From a note in Glassco's Journal, dated October, 1964.

[19] This was an "adaptation" by Glassco of a work by Ken Sato, an expatriate Japanese writer who had been living in Paris at the same time as Glassco, and who had

publisher, and in 1975, much to his credit, produced two major translations of French-Canadian writing: *Complete Poems of Saint Denys Garneau* and Monique Bosco's *La Femme de Loth* (*Lot's Wife*), which had won the Governor General's Award for fiction in 1971. Next, he took up Leopold von Sacher-Masoch's *Venus in Furs*,[20] which he promptly turned into another example of "adapted" erotica, publishing it with his introduction in 1977.

But, in spite of a more leisurely existence divided between Montreal and the Eastern Townships, that included escapes to warm climates in winter and even a return to Paris, Glassco's health was visibly in decline. His last project was a translation of Jean-Charles Harvey's ground-breaking novel *Les Demi-civilisés* (1934, 1962), which appeared posthumously under the title Glassco had wished for it: *Fear's Folly* (1982). He died on the 29th of January, 1981. Funeral services were held at The Church of St. James the Apostle (Anglican), the old family church at the corner of St. Catherine and Bishop Streets in Montreal. His ashes were placed in a stream that runs not far from his old house in Foster, Quebec.

Michael Gnarowski

---

published in 1928, "for private distribution" and in outlandish English, a collection of homosexual tales called *Quaint Stories of Samurais* which, according to Sato's introductory "Translator's Notes", had been selected and translated from the writings of the Japanese poet Saikaku Ibara (1641–1693). As his war-time correspondence with Robert McAlmon, the original but unidentified publisher of Sato's book, reveals, Glassco had had an eye on this material for some time. *The Temple of Pederasty* was published in paperback by Hanover House of Hollywood, California, and was stamped "Sale to Minors Prohibited". It had stylized illustrations conceived and commissioned by Glassco, and a suitably clandestine existence in that it was never widely distributed in Canada and, one is led to suspect, may even have been withdrawn from circulation.

[20]This was another piece of erotic writing with which Glassco had toyed for quite some time. He notes in his Journal on August 23rd, 1935 that a copy of *Venus in Furs* has arrived from New York. He says: "having got past Customs I don't know how." He also complained that the translation was a vile bit of work and the illustrations quite idiotic.

For Michael Gnarowski —
to swell his collection of Canadian pseudonyms,
this little item...
With kindest regards   John Glassco

26/vi/67

SQUIRE
HARDMAN

BY

GEORGE COLMAN

Reprinted from the Edition of 1871
with an Introduction by

JOHN GLASSCO

THE PASTIME PRESS
MCMLXVI

Titlepage of *Squire Hardman* (1966), privately published by Glassco in an
edition of fifty copies.

A Note on the Text

The text presented here is that of Glassco's *Selected Poems* (1971). There has been no editorial intrusion whatsoever into the body of the poetry. There is, however, some minor annotation stemming from the poems.

Additional matter that has been made part of this volume in order to provide a fuller sampling of Glassco's writing consists of excerpts from *Squire Hardman* (1966) and from *Montreal* (1973), as well as several translations of French-Canadian poetry and three short prose pieces that bear on the art of poetry and translation.

M.G.

1

THE RURAL MAIL

These are the green paths trodden by patience.
I hang on the valley's lip, a bird's eye viewing
All that opposes to makers and masters of nations
Only its fierce mistrust of the word—
To the smashed records for gobbling and spewing,
Cows that exist in a slow-motion world.

For here is man on man's estate of nature,
Farmer on farm, the savage civilized
Into the image of his God the weather—
Only another anarchist, foiled highflyer
Whose years have grown as a minute in his eyes,
Whose grin reveals a vision of barbed wire:

Here birth evokes pleasure and a reflective pity,
Marriage or mating, much of the voyeur,
Sickness, an interest and some hope of booty,
And death strikes like an oddly barked command,
Confounding with its *Easy*, its *As you were*,
His stiff-kneed generation unused to bend.

I sense his hours marked by my two-wheeled cart
Descending the stony hill: as I stop by his box
The ring of tin as the *Knowlton News* goes in
Is a day's knell—and the countryside contracts
For an instant to the head of a pin;
Or he comes with a money-order, or to chat.

Getting good money, and money is always good,
We keep the high standards in the front parlour
Like a wedding-cake or a motto carved in wood,
The falling-out of enemies makes no friends.
'Far as I'm concerned, the war can go on forever!'
A man can *make* a dollar, with hens.

25

Scraping the crumbling roadbed of this strife
With rotten fenceposts and old mortgages
(No way of living, but a mode of life),
How sift from death and waste three grains of duty,
O thoughts that start from scratch and end in a dream
Of graveyards minding their own business?

But the heart accepts it all, this honest air
Lapped in green valleys where accidents will happen!
Where the bull, the buzz-saw and the balky mare
Are the chosen fingers of God for a farmer's sins,
Like the axe for his woods, and his calves and chicks
   [and children
Destined for slaughter in the course of things.

————
————

STUD GROOM

Your boy's-ambition was to be a Horseman,
Some day to hear tell or overhear your name
Linked with that word. This was the foreseen
Reward for the five years in the dealer's stable,
For strewing your childhood nightly under his horses' feet
And bearing it out at sun-up on a shovel,

When you met all claims with waiver and deferment,
And learned the habit of not coming to grips
With any unhaltered thing that's not dependent
On a boy's will like a pious man on God's,
Till language lapsed back into clucks and chirps,
Hisses and heeyahs, steady-babes, be-goods.

And now it has all come true! and the mountains spill
Your world of cousins, a chorus of witnesses:
Lost Nation, Bolton Centre and Pigeon Hill

Acclaim you who combine, deny and defer
With straps and stalls the heats and the rampancies,
And the act that's blessed with a bucket of cold water.

Well, there is the World, in the attitude of approval,
Hands in its pockets, hat over its eyes,
Ignorant, cunning, suave and noncommittal,
The ape of knowledge. . . . Say, through what injustice
Has it gained the bounty, by what crazy process
Those eyes fell heir to your vision of success?

For the goal has changed — It's rather to have made
Of the welcoming music of nickers and whinnies
At feeding time, the brightness of an eye
Fixed on a bucket, the fine restraint of a hoof
Raised and held in a poised meaningless menace,
To have made, of these, assurances of love,

And of the denial of all loving contact
When the ears flatten, the eye rolls white,
The whirring alarm that keeps the dream intact
For poet and pervert too, whose spasm or nightmare
Makes, with the same clean decision of a bite,
Divorce between possession and desire.

For 'one woman leads to another, like one war
Leads to another,' and the fever has no end
Till passion turns — from the bright or bloody star,
From the bitter triumph over a stranger's body,
To something between a deity and a friend,
To a service halting between cult and hobby,

And nothing is left for the family or the nation
But a genial curse, and silence. It may be
You are the type of figures long out of fashion,
The Unknown Soldier and the Forgotten Man,
Whom the rest might envy, now, their anonymity
And the fact they were at least left alone;

And who might have said, like you, to a pair
Of nags looking over a sagging roadside fence,
Good Morning, girls! O greeting washed in air,
O simple insistence to affirm the Horse,
While the Loans and bomb-loads are hitting new highs
And youth is deducted at the source.

For 'Horseman, what of the future?' is a question
Without a meaning: there is always another race,
Another show, the unquenchable expectation
Of ribbons, the easy applause like a summer storm,
And the thrill, like love, of being in first place
For an instant that lasts forever, and does no harm

Except to the altar-fated passion it robs,
The children it cheats of their uniforms and wars,
And the fathomless future of the underdog
It negates — shrugs off like the fate of a foundered mare —
As it sparks the impenetrable lives, like yours
Whose year revolves around the county fair.

THE ENTAILED FARM

A footpath would have been enough.
The muddy mile of side-road has no purpose
Save as it serves for others to link up
Crossroads marked on the map with a nameless cross
By way of these choked and heartless fields of paintbrush
And the mute, sealed house,

Where the spring's tooth, stripping shingles, scaling
Beam and clapboard, probes for the rot below
Porch and pediment and blind bow-window,
And the wooden trunk with the coloured cardboard lining

Lies where it fell when the wall of the flying wing
Fell down ten years ago;

Where the stone wall is a haven for snake and squirrel,
The steepled dovecote for phoebe and willow-wren,
And the falling field-gates, trigged by an earthen swell,
Open on a wild where nothing is raised or penned,
On rusty acres of witch-grass and wild sorrel
Where the field-birds cry and contend.

You, tourist, salesman, family out for a picnic,
Who saw the bearded man that walked like a bear,
His pair of water-pails slung from a wooden neckyoke,
Slipping in by the woodshed — Come away,
That naked door is proof against all knocking!
Standing and knocking there,

You might as well expect time's gate to open
On the living past, the garden bloom again,
The house stand upright, hay-barn's swayback coping
Stiffen, and see as in a fretted frame
Men in the meadow and a small boy whooping
The red oxen down that orchard lane,

Or revive the slow strong greed of the coffined farmer
Who cleared, stumped, fenced, rotating sinew and sweat,
Beating the ploughshare into an honest dollar,
Who living and dying planned to cheat time's night
Through the same white-bearded boy — who is hiding
  [somewhere
Now, till you're out of sight,

And have left him alone: alone with the grief or anger
Or whatever it is that flickers but will not die
In the dull brain of the victim turned avenger,
At war with a shadow, in flight from passers-by,
From us — who are free from all but the hint of attainder,
Who can meet a stranger's eye

With a good face, can answer a question, give a reason,
For whom the world's fields and fences stand up plain,
Nor dazzle in sunlight or crumble behind the rain:
From us, with our hearts but lightly tinged with poison,
Who composed our quarrel early and in good season
Buried the hatchet in our father's brain.

GENTLEMAN'S FARM

Ten miles from anywhere eighty years and more,
Where the frozen roadstones grind iron shoes and tires
    And the timberwood's last stand
Lives only in brushwood and long memories — see,
The new-peeled posts are marching, the taut wires
    Sing to the naked land,

Sing to the valley of slash and beaver-meadow,
The stone-pocked fields and bog-born stunted alders
    And the black hills rising sheer
As mountains of iron and sand round the Genie's castle
(The age-old view of eyes that each November
    Look back on a wasted year),

That things are humming, that even here at last
The lights are going on, the wheels going round
    As the wasteland fulfils
The singular purpose, powered and glorified
Of the weekday absentee whose will has broken
    Between these barren hills,

And where the regional serf, time out of mind,
Morning and evening, blind with sweat and fury,
    Hollaed his shaggy tyke

After the peaked-arse cows in the hummocky pasture
Till they buckjumped to the dislocated barn,
    Their slack bags black with muck,

The silos rise and the cupolas of chrome,
Minarets of the mosque, the milkwhite temple
    Gleaming below the hill —
And look, by the mailbox winks the coloured legend,
Hillsview Farm, the Home of Reg'd Holsteins
    Stamped on a plaque of steel.

What passion is this? What fancy fed with tractors,
Engines and rancho-fence and palisades?
    Not here, at least,
Has the urban dream flowered in a homing impulse
Towards the inane, imagined verities
    In the soil, the dung, the teats —

Things of an island whose longed-after earth
The city of Columbus, falling on his knees,
    Kisses and calls it Saviour,
Making his garden where he can, his plea
Against the unreal tenures which enrage
    A street-begotten fever —

No, this is a dream-barn, a body of wood and iron
Figuring forth on the mind's wilderness,
    With wealth for an ally,
The structural mania of the human heart —
Whose buildings rise in a kinder soil than this,
    And beneath an inward eye

Where all goes well and the pioneer has profit,
Where the titan's work subserves as in a dream
    The all too fictive goal,
And the end is perfect beauty, the blessed vision,
The working out of a man's reverie
    Of his own memorial!

But here, while the eternal mountains stand,
Immortal stones come up beneath the plough,
    This valley's sun and rain
Score harshly and the bitter autumnal crop,
Scratched out with a hoe or shovelled by machines,
    Is still the same:

O forefixed harvest of man's reverie driven
Into the light of day and life of men,
    You bring the same revenge
On the impresarios of all sacred sweetness,
Whose eyes shall wake to witness, spring by spring,
    The sad and stealing change,

Hope battered into habit, and a habit
Running to weariness — the proof and process
    Of powers which must equate
Farmer and Gentleman through their monuments,
Till time's mathematic of indifference
    Confound them, to create

Not the bare living nor the orgulous legend
(Improbable flowers from seed of sweat or treasure),
    But what's more tenuous still,
A feast for the idler and the ragamuffin,
A more conspicuous waste of all endeavour
    That has had its will —

A common loveliness! — Look backward now,
As we breast the rubbly hill to the rotting sawmill,
    Back to the shining roof
That parries the pale farflung November sunlight
On lightning rods and the stammering weathervane
    Of a gilded calf:

See that the wreck of all things made with hands
Being fixed and certain, as all flesh is grass,
    The grandiose design

Must marry the ragged thing, and of the vision
Nothing endure that does not gain through ruin
   The right, the wavering line.

DESERTED BUILDINGS
UNDER SHEFFORD MOUNTAIN

These native angles of decay
   In shed and barn whose broken wings
Lie here half fallen in the way
Of headstones amid uncut hay —
   Why do I love you, ragged things?

What grace unknown to any art,
   What beauty frailer than a mood
Awake in me their counterpart?
What correspondence of a heart
   That loves the failing attitude?

Here where I grasp the certain fate
   Of all man's work in wood and stone,
And con the lesson of the straight
That shall be crooked soon or late
   And crumble into forms alone,

Some troubled joy that's half despair
   Ascends within me like a breath:
I see these silent ruins wear
The speaking look, the sleeping air
   Of features newly cast in death,

Dead faces where we strive to see
   The signature of something tossed
Between design and destiny,
Between God and absurdity,
   Till, harrowing up a new-made ghost,

We half embrace the wavering form,
   And half conceive the wandering sense
Of some imagined part kept warm
And salvaged from the passing storm
   Of time's insulting accidents.

So I, assailed by the blind love
   That meets me in this silent place,
Lift open arms: Is it enough
That restless things can cease to move
   And leave a ruin wreathed in grace,

Or is this wreck of strut and span
   No more than solace for the creed
Of progress and its emmet plan,
Dark houses that are void of man,
   Dull meadows that have gone to seed?

THE WHITE MANSION[1]

I am a bright thing on my rising ground,
A green hill behind me, a blue brook at my feet.
The dawn reddens my eastern doors,
The whirling sun makes my windows a glory.
The woods around me a hundred years ago
Were felled to raise my naked arms.
Ere I was done the hairy pioneer
Fell dead exulting in his dream.
I am the death of man and of his dream.

I am a homestead in a hundred acres:
I draw them round me and devour them.
I eat the farmer's flesh and his children
—Who but I hollaed the sweating team?—

Their hands were worn away in my service,
Sold my acres one by one to strangers.
Ere I was done the dying farmer cursed me,
Crying within the strangling noose of hope.
I am the grave of the husbandman's hope.

I am a shining temple, a tall man's pride.
My groves are planted with plumy pines.
Through my avenues of cedar, my stone pillars,
Fly slender horses, tracery of wheels.
My lights were seen all through the summer night.
Within and without he dressed me in splendour.
Ere I was done I stripped him naked,
Sent him away weeping, to beg for money.
I am the dancer blown with tears and money.

I am the fairest court of love and pleasure.
My hedges tangle, my lawn return to hay;
The woods crept up to my rotted door-sills,
Stones fell in, but ever amid the mouldering walls
The holy fire streamed upright on the altar:
Two hearts, two bodies clove, knew nothing more.
Ere I was done I tore them asunder. Singly
They fled my ruin and the ruin of love.
I am she who is stronger than love.

I shall never be done: no man shall see it.
My brightness overtops his dream.
I am the scourge of hope: I bury my servants.
I am the sink of wealth: behold my trees.
I am the tomb of love: the altar is broken.
Swan-white I float among bare crusted maples.
Grey hills behind me, black water at my feet,
I await the stroke from which I shall arise
To announce once more the death of man.

John Glassco

THE BRILL ROAD

Skeletons of scarecrows, buoys for the sailor of snow,
The broomhead sticks of brush tell where it goes
Straight into a white screaming sky
Of tons of a snowblind wind scouring like sand
The walls of the last valley-house in the half-light,
Where its lap would be if the mountain were a man.

And the mare looks back: are we going upwards, master?
Yes, we follow the blinding years,
Into the sweeping, swallowing wind,
Into the gape of all and the loss of the person
Driving his birthright deathward in a trance
Over the mountain's swollen Jovian brow,

Like a mind grappling with its own betrayal,
Thoughts thinning out, the basis crumbling,
Rising, rising ever into more breathless air
And a frailer tenure, while the wind blows,
The hills darken, and this heaven-riving road thrown
Like a noosed lifeline to five worthless farms
Peters out under the snow.

The road is a trick, like every form of life,
A signal into the dark impartial storm
(The leveller of land, the old mound-maker
Smoother of great and small): though the road is wrong
Always, and leads upwards forever
To impossible heights, into the boiling snow,
There is no turning back; but the road is a trap.

This is the involvement that we never sought.
How should we know its conditions, terms
Determined by the swollen alien brow?
Only we do the mountain's bidding, while the storm
Beats in our eyes, exhausts our servants,
Tearing the robe from knee and shoulder,
Making a terrible half-light of our day.

And from this day we drive into the trap,
Seeking the mountain, the five worthless farms.
Do we move to a screaming music, is that all?
What is this orchestra of fear? Absurd
Are the equations for us and our servants
Madly seeking the other side of the mountain.
Does it even exist, that quiet road
Snow-pleached between the laden, bending trees
Where the small, fat birds will be flitting and feeding,
Where the wind is muffled and we move at peace?

―――――――――

THE BURDEN OF JUNK

April again, and its message unvaried, the same old
    [impromptu
Dinned in our ears by the tireless dispassionate
    [chortling of Nature,
Sunlight on grey land, the grey of the past like a
    [landscape around us
Caught in its moment of nakedness also, a pitiful
    [prospect
Bared to the cognitive cruelty shining upon it: O
    [season,
Season that leads me again, like this road going
    [over the mountain,
Past the old landmarks and ruins, the holdfasts of
    [hope and ambition—

Why is the light doubly hard on the desolate
    [places? why even
Hardest of all on the tumbledown cabin of Corby
    [the Trader?
See, with its tarpaper hanging in tatters, the
    [doorstep awash in a

Puddle of cow-piss and kindling-chips, ringed with
　　[the mud of a fenceless
Yardful of rusty and broken machinery, washstands
　　[and bedsteads,
Bodies of buggies and berlots, the back seats of
　　[autos, bundles of
Chicken-wire, leaves of old wagon-springs and
　　[miscellaneous wheels. ... But

There is Corby himself in the mud and the sunshine,
　　[in front of the
Lean-to cowshed, examining something that looks
　　[like a sideboard,
Bidding me stop and admire, and possibly make
　　[him an offer:
'Swapped the old three-teated cow for a genuine
　　[walnut harmonium!
Look, ain't a scratch or a brack in it anywhere —
　　[pedals and stopples
Work just as good as a fellow could ask for! Over
　　[to Broome they
Say they used to cost four hundred dollars apiece
　　[from the factory ... '

Here is the happy collector of objects, the absolute
　　[type of
All who engage in the business of buying and
　　[shifting, the man who
Turns a putative profit into an immediate pleasure,
Simply by adding a zero to his account with a self-
　　[owned
Bank of Junk, and creates a beautiful mood of
　　[achievement
Out of nothing at all! Ah here is the lord of the
　　[cipher,
This is the Man of the Springtime, the avatar of
　　[Lyaeus![2]

We should be trading indeed, if we could, I think
  [as I leave him.
Mine is a burden of lumber that ought to be left
  [with him also:
This is where it belongs, with the wheels and the
  [beds and the organ,
With all the personal trash that the spirit acquires
  [and abandons,
Things that have made the heart warm and
  [bewildered the senses with beauty
Long ago — but that weakened and crumbled away
  [with the passion
Born of their brightness, the loves that a dreary
  [process of dumping
Leaves at last on a hillside to rot away with the
  [seasons.

———————

THE ART OF MEMORY

But is it so, as one remembers Carthage
who has seen it? No.
  —ST AUGUSTINE, *Confessions*, X, 19

To be awake today is to be warned.
The unwrinkled lake, the landscape and the leaves
Shimmered all morning, sails and yellow flowers
Dragging another glory from the dead.

The sun of noon, annunciator, struck:
An hour returning from another world.
Blink! go the eyes, in the middle of it all,
Wanting Athene's shield of glassy brass;

Wanting the paradisal past's intenser light,
My eyelids burn: this hour's page

Is a blur of words, and every word in flames. .... Oh then
Alas for all familiar things and thoughts,
For the clear of vanished presences before me,

And for their meaning to me, here and now,
As only pegs and props, characters
In the fable of a being — oh infinitely
Remote: I mean, daffodils in a vase,
Sail on the water, sunlight on the grass.

So if no more, why then no more. The train
Of images romance drew in her wake
Like stars in water, troubled and yet true,
Those floating points that charmed a universe

To an idea of itself not wholly
Base, and impressed their fictions here and there —
Shine, fictions that are feelings, shine forever
In the blue aspect of Armance's eyes!

Sift now and handle that too-sacred dust,
And be its fool again, daring the holy deeps,
Having ado with desire, the dark stranger,
Playing with gods, the faces upon coins,

But all in game — the stake, as it was between
That pair of royal apes that ribbed Gonzalo,
A laughter, a waking-up! Till you too wake
And hear time itself talking:

'I am this day, this hour, that speaks: mine is
The smooth-tongued challenge of time saying,
I give you this hour, perfect, splendid, shining,
Spill it before you. Here it is at last:

Here is the empty frame, the gilded stage
Set for high deeds, adoration, what you will,
For happiness deferred, guarded so long:
I do my part. I show my hand. Take the key.'

And here is the dry light, the beach of stones.
Never will earth break open or god speak,
No Curtius mount and gallop
Full-armed into the public pit —

Only eyes closing, hooded from the sun,
Suffice in this splenetic hour to ease
The lust of matter, flagrat of dry bones
Sluiced with the humours of an afternoon,

When how to accept the blank of closing doors,
As saints and martyrs do their palms and pains,
Is the only question: to retrieve in desperation
What was rejected in despite: to see

Items as undiscoverable isles
And leave them so, with the accidental ocean
Laving their lambent whatness — to the sense
Inviolate, beyond geography,

And so much deeper by so far untouched
By hope or hunger. So I do, I do;
So leave them as they were, poised on the point
Of what they are this moment, and so resign
The flowers to yellow and the lake to blue.

———————

THE WHOLE HOG

When I was very young my mother told me
That my father was the strongest of men
(Not in words at first, of course — but I knew);
Later I learned he was the best and bravest;
And during my adolescence (a difficult
Time for us all) I had her whispered word for it
He was the wisest parent in the world.

Long ago I put aside the question
Of her motive in this matter. ... Perhaps
A sense of guilt for the disloyalty
Of a too-clear, too-wifely-valuation
Of his man's-worth, was expiated so:
Enough that I too now appreciate
The situation, and appraise the need.

For now I wonder about his part only,
Asking myself through just what consciousness
Of his own fragility the man was induced
To accept this grand vocation — as he did —
And dropping all else, set himself to become
Great God to a little child? It is a question
That opens up vistas of personal hell. ...

To be the Absolute to someone else:
Figure the concitations of the demon
That drove him to this! Like a hunted beast,
Like a starving man, like a falling stone,
He followed his blind will to its end in nature,
Projected himself into infinity
And silvered a looking-glass in his son's eye.

I try to guess what image haunted him,
What spectral littleness of man alone:
Paltry Invictus with the head of clay
Jabbered at him from the pools in his mind,
Loomed in the coalsacks of its sky, met him
At flowery turnings in his private garden,
In sleep, in love, at billiards, at the ball;

Until he must have realized that the world was
Not only too much with him, but too much for him —
For poor Invictus, the poor gentleman
Who laid claim, simply, to the whole universe,
But brought no vouchers, bore no strawberry mark!

And when lovely woman failed him, womanly,
He built an altar in the sands of my heart.

I have not sacrificed there for years ...
But the altar stands, eternal absolute,
As if its foundations were laid in living rock;
And when I went whoring after strange gods,
Why, they were Gods, and it was whoring still —
With reason, unreason, duality of will,
And many others, masks of Nobodaddy,

In my father's house there were no dissensions,
There, all was unanimity and family:
Now the plates fly in my head night and day;
There, was infallible authority:
Now I am free as a crow to fly or stay;
There, was no check nor doubt nor indecision:
Here I am a dog whistled by many masters,

Always obliged to go the whole hog,
And with no hambone even to drop in the water;
Nosing about the world for love and tid-bits
I am still baffled by the faith-breakings
Of flesh in season and sonorous language
That tell me I also am a piece of property
And rouse only my barking rhetoric in answer;

For experience only leads me about in a circle,
And learning by heart still leaves my heart rebellious
To the violent patterns, the makeshift morals
Whose insoluble equation leaves me as cold
As the by-blow baby left all night on the doorstep:
— That home with wealthy windows lit, is mine!

See the Portland vase before the Venetian mirror
In my father's house. It is filled with *honesty*.
The abstraction found its body long ago
In a plant of eternally dessicated leaves,

As my father's demons spoke of his hold forever
On my heart, and mine of the fragile tenure
Of all things: we have learned the porcine betrayals.

———————

QUEBEC FARMHOUSE

Admire the face of plastered stone
      The roof descending like a song
            Over the washed and anointed walls,
Over the house that hugs the earth
Like a feudal souvenir: oh see
The sweet submissive fortress of itself
            That the landscape owns!

And inside is the night, the airless dark
      Of the race so conquered it has made
            Perpetual conquest of itself,
Upon desertion's ruin piling
The inward desert of surrender,
Drawing in all its powers, puffing its soul,
            Raising its arms to God.

This is the closed, enclosing house
      That set its flinty face against
            The rebel children dowered with speech
To break it open, to make it live
And flower in the cathedral beauty
Of a pure heaven of Canadian blue —
            The larks so maimed

They still must hark and hurry back
      To the paradisal place of gray,
            The clash of keys, the click of beads,
The sisters walking leglessly,

While under the wealth and weight of stone
All the bright demons of forbidden joy
            Shriek on, year after year.

THE SCREAMING CHILD

Down under a grey stone wall, in the long grass
Starred with buttercups and daisies, the suntrap of summer
Feasted with the scent of warmed and minted green,
Ridden over by sun and cloud-led shadows,
The mother is rocking the screaming child in her arms.
                    Balow, my pretty babe, balow!

It is no use, young woman, cease your crying,
Vowing, caressing: all those tender words,
Moans of possession, shakes and trills of love,
Are wasted on this mud-eyed bawling morsel,
This growth of a moment's infection dredged from your loins
Into the pure air of summer: it knows, it knows —
Better than suffering's self in the hospital,
Prison, asylum, exile, furnished room —
The entrapment of its state, the plight, the prison.
Or smile if you wish, pour out your pity
In a protective passion like dirty dishwater
Over the shaken body and shrieking face
Of this little master of the atonal mode —
                    Balow, my pretty one, balow! —

But this is your doing and desire, the original
Object found, the awful thing made in our image
That must continue to the final chapter,
The last judgement, the paranoiac dream,
Crazed with liberty, freely projecting

Desire and delirium into a private world—
And what for that endless horror now?

Sing, rock and sing

Like Moll of Bedlam, that is all your blessed business,
To so immure this soul with music it may also
Forget the grinding wheel and the gaudy prize,
And make this moment of your motherkindness
The beginning of its melancholy art.

Balow, my pretty babe, balow!

———————
———————

A HOUSE IN THE COUNTRY

The crazy way in which it stands
Proclaims the house was built with hands;
Its gardens so long have wanted care
The flowers now seem intruders where
Priapus and Pomona were;
And both of them must be irate,
So fallen from their former state,
Their shrines broken and desolate,
To see how thistle, burdock, weed,
Flourish, flower and spread their seed.
Like broken furrows run the paths,
The gravel's overgrown with grass,
And half the grass is choked with moss;
The kitchen garden lies outspread
As if all gardeners were dead:
Those hidden, rotting cucumber frames
You'll trip over and break your shins;
This trailing arbour bears a vine
Whose grapes so bitter, bare and thin,
No miracle could turn to wine.

A timid tramp went by last night,
And at the staring sheep took fright:
The poor chilled devil as he ran
Cursed dogs as enemies of man—
And such an incident can please
When barge-lights in the shore-line trees
Are all that break our reveries.
And when the rains come on we'll set
Pans in the attic to catch the drip,
And watch the struggles soft moths make
Fast bound within the spider's web,
Or see the dangling spinner drop
To bind his prey, then kill and sup;
Admire his sturdy consort's knack
Of bearing the babies on her back;
Observe, too, as we see her bite
His head off in an amorous bout,
How love engenders appetite.

We have clean air, meat, cheese and ale
To keep our wits from growing stale,
And the occasional visitor
To remind us what our duties are.

LUCE'S NOTCH

Here's where the road ends, on this windy height
Over Bolton Wood, where fifteen years ago
I climbed one summer day, turned round and stopped
Amazed at the beauty of the valleys seen
From the stones of Luce's ruined doorway: then,
I would come back some day, I thought; and so
Turned my back to it and kept climbing on,

John Glassco

Walking beside my two-wheeled cart, while Phyllis
Plodded between the shafts, her chestnut flanks
Wrinkling, straining, her head between her knees,
As the road became a pathway, lost its face
In hummocks, boulders, chattering streams and then
Died in a thin flat meadow fenced with stones,
A place enclosed, where the surrounding slopes
Ran out so far the view was quite cut off;
And at the farther end a rutted gap
Gave on the ruins of a grassy lane,
Which following we at last came out and down
On the road to St. Etienne.

                Never again
Did I go that way, and never shall. The road
Is blocked now: see, not only choked with brush
And saplings, but inalterably sealed
By two half-hidden massive concrete cubes
Joined by a length of iron pipe: why not?
Who goes to St. Etienne? Or if he does
Who in his senses ever chose to go
These fifty years by way of Luce's Notch?

However that may be, whatever fool
I was in those days—for I often went
By curious ruined ways and roundabouts—
This is the road's end now, this stop the last;
From here the only way is turning back
To join the links of casual circles leading
Home, or somewhere else I have been before.
—The road is blocked, the chestnut mare is dead,
The cart is mouldering in the loft, and I
Stand here alone, seeing how on this height
That leans over the green gulf of Bolton Glen,
With the intervolved valleys locked in the haze
Of still midsummer, how on this dizzy height
Robin and swallow still fight against the wind

Blown from the mountain whose thin meadows run
Rippling into the sky — stand here again
Beside the wreck of Aaron Luce's barn,
Fronting the valley after fifteen years,
Seeing nothing that I did not see that day,
Feeling only the same despair before things
Still alien, still mysterious, still removed.

There is no outward change: the silvery barn,
All that is left of the work of Luce's hands,
Still stands, tilted at the same angle of falling
It had then (for the buildings hereabouts
Are long in standing, longer still in falling,
And wear for a man's lifetime the final grace
Of tottering and attrition like a crown);
Nothing has changed in all this quiet scene,
And least of all where — not so far above
Eye-level now, across the trough of green —
Old Foster lifts his round and ruined head
Into the sky, a mound of wrinkled stone
Sprinkled with thin white birches.
                              Ah, but now
Mounted as high as this above the world,
And higher still above all things comprising
The round of living — memories, affections,
The daily tasks and duties, so much of the earth
As binds us to it, inexorably dear! —
Now, if at any time, I should resolve
The secret of that despair, should understand
Why all things radiant and remote in nature —
The fields, the woods, the waterfalls and rocks,
And scenes like this, the valley's green expanse
Seen from the stones of Luce's ruined doorway —
Bring me, as ever, a feeling close to tears.

In earlier days I thought I knew the spring
Of that ecstatic suffering which is joy,

That sense of being unable to possess
A natural scene, or be possessed by it,
That grief engendered by the desperate wish
To make such moments last forever, to stop
Time's hands and the very passage of the blood,
Freeze every conscious faculty, and then —
In a reversal of the course whereby,
As with the loves of saints, desire itself
Is made through the alchemy of their God's grace
The mode of some diviner discontent —
Let all my shapeless flame of yearning change,
Harden and materialize into the form
Of sensual appetite: in those days, indeed,
There seemed one reason only for this pain:
Its end was in its beginning, it was only
In the same rank as the natural affections,
An aspect of inordinate desire.

    This madness I have no more. I only see
Beauty continues, and so do not I.
I have become an ageing eye through which
A young man looks again and trembles, lost
To his own present — and he had no past —
For all his future is what I have become,
A man on a mountain after fifteen years,
A man implicit in that careless heart
Even then when all his idle study was
To drive about the hills in search of strangeness,
Seeking he knew not what, and now has found
Here on this windy height — his wandering loves
Come home to importune him with sorrow now
And fill this foolish ageing child of his
With the sense of what is always failing, fleeting,
Falling away into the gulf of time.
Was it so strong, that careless idle heart?
Do I exist entirely in that man?
A man's identity is never certain,

And least of all my own: today it seems
My whole existence is a pointless dream
Beneath old Foster's blind, tree-sprinkled head;
I am a breath, a nothing, an illusion,
A foolish brain jailed in a creaking skull,
With neither youth nor age, nor any time
To be or to become, so speed the seasons
That waste my substance in these lovely places.
And yet not wholly so; for still I feel
That these green fields, these waterfalls and woods,
These valleys and these winding roads that follow
Always the heights — no matter at what length,
Time being nothing to the men who made them! —
That all these things which now are quite confused
In a beautiful composite of man and nature,
So that even old Foster seems to bless
The farms spread out beneath his weightless shadow,
That they, who are made to outlast my span of vision,
And in whose life the glimpses that I gain
Of the mute, breathing beauty of the world
Stand as a passing moment only, a blink
Between me and the everlasting darkness,
May come to consciousness through me.

                                    Therefore,
You natural scenes to whose eternity
My transient vision and my life are bound,
Teach me to see: give me eyes all over
To multiply the adoration that is in me
For all your insensate parts, for every stone,
For every little watercourse that runs
Between its alders and forget-me-nots,
Daisy and wild rose; keep me as I am now,
Here on this solitary mountain-top,
Purged of each last impulsion of desire
To make you mine, to carry you along
On the wings of possession! Let me be:

Release me from the lust of wanting, grant me
This sadness always, continuance of this vision;
Stay with me, sorrow that is not sorrow but
The spring of all delight, of the troubled joy
Wherein I approach the consciousness of things
Yearning and aching always, and so become
Each day more closely bound to what you are.

NEEDHAM CEMETERY

'A sightly place,' says Luke Orlando Ball
In *The History of Brome County*, 'sandy of soil,
Easy of access, level and well-drained.
You never saw the dead so well maintained.'
— Never, indeed: here corpses seldom spoil

Even in the wettest year — and this means much
To folk who raise their eyes to heaven but keep
Their feet upon the dear familiar ground
Which wears them out, as they go round and round
And to and fro: a kind of thinking sheep.

So slow to grasp, they like the second look,
So short of sight, they favour the long view;
And all that happens is that, right or wrong,
One comes too late, the other takes too long:
Time led them here, as it was bound to do. . . .

As it was bound to do. And still the dead
Lecture their children on the way to live;
For the blood's didactic can perpetuate
Their useless virtues which are out of date,
Their antique vices which we half forgive.

Draw close, lean down, let the communal voice
Of a long-buried elder testify
Out of the soil he thought of first and last
(Bating his little leisure, which was passed
In waiting for his enemies to die):

'Mind your own business. Owe no man a cent.
Keep out of trouble and away from war.
Don't trust a Frenchman. Be nobody's fool:
Nothing for nothing is the golden rule;
God lives in walls, the devil keeps the door.

'Look to the end. Pride goes before a fall.
The one mistake, remember, is to grow
Too big for your breeches: that's where Agag dulled
And how the tipsy Amalekites got fooled;
Jezebel flew high: she landed low.

'All flesh is grass: so keep the meadows up,
The hired man down, the women in their place;
Let your whole life turn with the turning year,
Obedient to the seasons. Have no fear
Lest hardness hood your eyes or twist your face,

'For sweet goes bad, but sour goes on forever ...
So look at your feet, your fields, the things you own,
And find God's meaning there: cows in the barn,
Crop in the mow and taxes paid. The farm,
The farm is the whole of life — what death alone

'Can take from you, giving himself instead
In whom its guardian and its genius move,
So interwoven is the daily round
— Dust in the air and silence underground —
That out of him you make your second love.'

Such counsels of perfection I have heard
In the autumn wind that sighs above these stones
Covered with angels, roses, pointing hands,

Witnessing what life gives and death demands
On a dry hillside full of farmers' bones.

———————
———————

CATBIRD[3]

For Marian Scott

'Airoee...
eh 'rhehu 'vrehu
eh villia villia 'vrehu, eh villia 'vrehu
    eh velù villiu villiu villiu!
'tse dàigh   dàigh   dàigh
'tse-de-jay 'tse-de-jay 'tsee-'tsee 'tsìrritse-'tsìrritse
        'tsirao 'twitsee
'wìtitsee 'wètitsee wètitsee wit'yu woity woity woity
téeah wéeah, te-wéeah-weeàh
k'tuf à tuf à tuf à tuf à tuf à te kerry
k'rry k'rry k'rry, tú!
ka 'kea kowa, keka keka!
'tw'ait, tw'it. Tw'at.

Cràow! 'Tsh'àow!

Quèah? Pueàh!
soit soit soit, twee twee 'twittitsee
kooka prea prea prea, preoi, preait, preoit,
      preeai preoo, pirriweet, peto peto peto

Pràigh! Pràigh!
Pip te waigh à tshewa
pip te woi wee, 'tshippewatt 'wurr-wurr.

Sooteet   sooteet   sooteet

'*airoee? airoee* . . .
Cr'àow! Tsh'àow!

'tship.

_____

_____

_____

2

THE CARDINAL'S DOG[4]

(Musée d'Autun)

The unknown Master of Moulins
Painted the Nativity: we see
The stable, the stupid ox and Mary,
Simpering Joseph on his knees
And the Cardinal Rolin on his knees too,
His red robe centred by a rat-faced dog.

They all look at each other: Joseph at Mary,
Mary (her face is blue) at the child,
The Cardinal looks, if anywhere, at the ox;
But the child looks at the little dog,
And the dog at nothing, simply being well-behaved:
He is the one who feels and knows ...

Pensive little dog (you that I love
Being only flesh and blood) you see
The reason for all this, the dying need
Of the worshipful, the master: so
We are all one, have seen the birth of God

Either through eyes of friend or master,
In a book, a song, a landscape or a child,
For a breath of time are immortal, tuned
To the chord and certainties of animal hope.
And the picture *teaches us* — as Balzac would say —
To trust anything on earth more than man.

———————
———————

59

John Glassco

THOMAS À KEMPIS

His unsubsistent mind, self-moving and
Subject to *rerum horror*, could observe
— Before its descent into the nightly grave —
Not that the cell expands, but the prisoner
Diminishes himself, not that he's brave,
But that, on earth, there's nothing left to fear.
Nobodaddy held him in his hand,

A fireless particle. I think we are
Coals ever cooling, blown at times by God;
And whether to strike or suffer for the good
Of all that breath has meant divides my hours,
And though to strike, to inch the door abroad,
Is all my vision allows (that — merciful powers! —
Confounds the firefly and the falling star),

The stroke or sufferance in the midnight is
An orchestral sigh. Always the cell is here,
Stronger than fire, than the release of fear,
Than any love that I can answer for. ...
But oh, green leaves and singing birds that see
The flaming sun, lie, lie of the open door,
The air of that bright heaven that is not his!

UTRILLO'S WORLD

I

He sat above it, watching it recede,
A world of love resolved to empty spaces,
Streets without figures, figures without faces,
Desolate by choice and negative from need.
But the hoardings weep, the shutters burn and bleed;
Colours of crucifixion, dying graces,
Spatter and cling upon these sorrowful places.
— Where is the loved one? Where do the streets lead?

There is no loved one. Perfect fear
Has cast out love. And the streets go on forever
To blest annihilation, silently ascend
To their own assumption of bright points in air.
It is the world that counts, the endless fever,
And suffering that is its own and only end.

II

Anguished these sombre houses, still, resigned.
Suffering has found no better face than wood
For its own portrait, nor are tears so good
As the last reticence of being blind.
Grief without voice, mourning without mind,
I find your silence in this neighbourhood
Whose hideous buildings ransom with their blood
The shame and the self-loathing of mankind.

They are also masks that misery has put on
Over the faces and the festivals:
Madness and fear must have a place to hide,
And murder a secret room to call his own.
I know they are prisons also, these thin walls
Between us and what cowers and shakes inside.

John Glassco

BRUMMELL⁵ AT CALAIS

A foolish useless man who had done nothing
All his life long but keep himself clean,
Locked in the glittering armour of a pose
Made up of impudence, chastity and reserve—
How does his memory still survive his world?

The portraits show us only a tilted nose,
Lips full blown, a cravat and curly wig,
And a pair of posturing eyes,
Infinitely vulnerable, deeply innocent,
Their malice harmless as a child's:

And he has returned to childhood now, his stature
That of the Butterfly whose *Funeral*
He sang (his only song) for one of his
Dear duchesses, Frances or Georgiana,
In the intolerable metre of Tom Moore—

To a childhood of sweet biscuits and curaçao;
Hair-oil and tweezers make him forget his debts,
The angle of his hat remains the same,
His little boots pick their way over the cobblestones,
But where is he going as well as going mad?

Nowhere: his glory is already upon him,
The fading Regency man who will leave behind
More than the ankle-buttoning pantaloon!
For see, even now in the long implacable twilight,
The triumph of his veritable art,

An art of being, nothing but being, the grace
Of perfect self-assertion based on nothing,
As in our vanity's cause against the void
He strikes his elegant blow, the solemn report of those
Who have done nothing and will never die.

FANTAISIES D'HIVER

After Théophile Gautier[6]

I

In sable, stoat and miniver
   The women walk beneath the trees;
A winter costume also decks
   Each goddess of the Tuileries.

Venus Rising from the Sea
   Has a pelisse with hood and ruff,
And Flora, bullied by the breeze,
   Keeps her hands within her muff.

And Coysevox'[7] and Coustou's[8] girls!
   The shepherdesses, one expects,
Have found the season cold for scarves
   And wrapped those boas round their necks.

II

The North has thrown its heavy load
Of mantles on the Paris mode,
As if a hairy Scythian laid
His bearskin on a Grecian maid:

Everywhere the finery
Palmyra wears in January
Blends with a Russian pomp of fur
Perfumed with Indian vetiver.

And in the alcove Pleasure laughs
To see, among the naked Loves,
How Venus' shoulders white and bare
Rise from a wild beast's rufous hair!

III

Though you keep safe from jealous eyes
    The features which your veil conceals,
If you walk out in snow like this,
    Beware those Andalusian heels!

The snow is taking little casts
    Of both your feet: so bear in mind
With every step along the street
    You leave your signature behind,

A trail the surly Husband may
    Follow, and find the secret hold
Where Psyche gives herself to Love
    With cheeks still rosy from the cold.

BELLY DANCE

The corpsewhite column spiralling on slow feet
Tracing the seashell curve, the figure eight,
Coldly unwinds its flowing ribbon
With public motions of the private psalm
Of supposed woman to the thought of man;

And like that man of Bierce's[9] wrestling
In the embrace of an invisible Thing,
Flaps in snakehead-strike doublejointed death —
An evocation of circumfluent air,
The adversary in a breath of air.

And the air is icy. Love, that is violence
Made easy, is here the end of all, a dance,
And man the viewless form, the animal
No longer animal but seeing-eye,
But super-member of impossible man.

So the man of air supplants the man of bone,
And it is he who writhes before a glass,
Before the figure of his only love,
The viewless member in his nerveless hand
Working within the adverse air.

———————

THE DEATH OF DON QUIXOTE

I

So this is what it is,
The world of things, arrested.
The music in my brain has stopped.
The armies are simply sheep, the giants windmills,
Dulcinea a cow-girl,
Mambrinus' helmet a barber's basin —
And the priest is delighted,
Fussing over me as I lie here
After my marvellous interminable journeys,
Shorn of my armour, extenuated,
Now in my five wits, restored,
Ready to make a good death.
— Rosinante and Dapple are dead too
Where are their bones?

Are we all as dead as my Amadis
Who slew so many giants, indomitable?
I who modelled my endeavour, who tried ...

Yes, this is what it is to be alive,
To die, to cease
To force a folly on the world.

II

The trees beyond the window are blowing green
The long road white in the distance, the sunshine,
There are flowers at my window
What do I know?

Well, that nothing partakes of reality,
And I too am simply Alonso Quixano the Good,
The wise gentleman, the restored,
Lying in my bed, tended
By my loving people, ready
To make a good death ...

I appear to have killed myself
By believing in some other God:
Or perhaps it was the drubbings did for me,
The horseplay, the jokes
Wore out my silly casing of flesh.
In any event, as I lie here,
The withdrawal of the vision,
The removal of the madness,
The supplanting of a world of beauty
By God's sticks and stones and smells
Are afflictions, I find, of something more absurd
Than any book of chivalry.

III

O my God
I have lost everything
In the calm of my sanity
Like a tree which regards itself
In still water
Seeing only another tree,
Not as when the crazy winds of heaven blew
Turning it to a perpetual fountain
Of shaken leaves,

The image of an endless waltz of being
So close to my heart I was always asking
Why should we not dance so for ever, be always
Trees tossed against the sky?
Why are we men at all if not to defy
This painted quietude of God's world?

Well, everything must have an end.
I have had my day
I have come home
I see things as they are.
My ingenious creator has abandoned me
With the insouciance of a nobleman
The fickleness of an author
The phlegm of an alguazil —

Only Sancho is faithful unto death
But in his eyes I discern the terrible dismay
For he sees that mine are at last a mirror of his own.

———————
———————

FLY IN AUTUMN

Here he is, the loathsome one
Pushing from a crack in the window,
Fat with unseasonable seed, making his way
Towards the light of the dying year,

Washing his hands wearily, bemused
By the fictive summer of the house,
Driven from sleep by his god,
Feeling for his destiny.

Where are his parents, those spry lechers
Of a summer of roses and wine?
Papery corpses crumbling. Their bloated child
Stalks the failing sun.

Beelzebub, Prince of this World,
Is this not your servant in whom you were well pleased,
Now beloved of none, and sick?
Worthless one, Prince of this World ...

Maggot, call on a greater god today:
Mercy, mercy, avert your lethal finger!
Let me but live to suffer the frost,
The slower death accessible to all.

———————
———————

FOR CORA LIGHTBODY, R.N.

You are a landscape in the Tale of Terror,
    Ca. 1910. Your bibful of breasts secrete
    Those dreamy fields, fens, fells, that sinister street
Of the Georgian nightmare I must love forever,
Where up in the attic, or hunched behind a mirror,
    Now in a cloud, now in a winding-sheet,
    The Thing is lurking; cling your palpably sweet
Lips to mine, softly as all that sugary horror.

And your one hour is the evening of the ending
    When under a sky like the breast of a dove
The dénouement climbs the creaking staircase. — Blood!
    Shots, screams, italics!
                In a spasm like my spending
The Foul Thing drops; in you, my hospital love,
    I sink my shaft as in auriferous mud.

———————
——————————
———————

3

A DEVOTION: TO CTEIS

Well, I shall kneel, that the whole world can say
Here is desire too that has come to pray.
The poles of pleasure in our divided dust
Meet often in their own tropics, lust and lust,
Devotion and devotion, but to join
Either to other is this way of mine;
Here to confound the order that's been planned
In man's imagined globe, the seas and land
Huddle together, make fire from beneath
Burst on his Arctic, and in the rotten teeth
Of all his moralist-geographers
Hurl nature in his embrace, and mine in hers!
Now when my mouth, that holds my heart, has become
An infinite reverence's ciborium,
Now, when the surcharged spiritual part
Exhales its burden—marvel, O marvel at
This joining, this economy of love
That turns the pious breath, the gesture of
My extreme adoration to a kiss,
As if it were all that could be made of this!

—Soon, soon begins the long intense journey
My lips shall lead you and my care delay,
But ere we embark, and ere thou shalt—O stay!—
Translate thy vision, seeing through closed eyes
The ideal form of carnal ecstasies;
Ere thou'rt become all sensible, and I
Am grown a very incubus thereby,
Oh let us hang, as the waves of ocean do,
An instant in the arrest of what we travel to.

See, I'd not slip from worshipper into man
A space yet, but remain as I began,

71

Give my lips holiday from the work of words,
Sabbath of silence, drifting pleasurewards,
And let my spirit, as my knees do, bow
Before this cloven idol—an altar now
As the old speechless misremembered year
Returns in noonlight, hunger and rage and fear
Cancelled forever, and as there bloom in me,
On the bare branches of my cynic tree,
Like mistletoe run wild, the devotee,
The lover and the child.

THE WEB

Fronting the sea that hungers for my man,
Bending my slanting eyes on the grey-gold web,
Here am I happy: what joy have other women
Like to my joy? What perfectness of pleasure?
Now it is mine, the part of a very goddess
As I weave and unweave the gleaming colours, my triumph,
In the face of the suitors and a son's unavailing anger!
I Penelope, fronting the sea and the birds flying,
Stir the discord, see the broil of men.

And O the lovely broil, the ruin, my pleasure,
The marvellous stir and strife of the suitors
And the shame of the house they turn to a jangling brothel!

Turn, desire and greed, to your reeling folly,
As I fool now one, now the other, flaunting the web,
And lie alone in the bed he hewed from the olive!
Only Athene I fear, and a bird flying left—
Only the piercing glance, and the omen.
She, she alone, a goddess, sees my heart.

My son is locked from my heart: like his lickpenny father
He counts the brown beeves, the yellow wine-jars.
He is cunning, but not with his father's seer-sight,
And wise, but not with his mother's wisdom,
Wisdom learned from the weight of a liar's shoulders
In the bed he hewed, O a thief and a liar always.
Does Athene see it, the grey-eyed glance
Pierce to my pleasure? No, I trust the sea!
Zeus, keep him upon the hungry sea forever

While I bend my eyes again on the sea and the grey-gold web,
On the sign of all things, my endless pleasure,
A woman's triumph, the gleaming tissue of discord
Woven of the broil of men and the shame of a house
Turned to a brothel, a place of reeling folly,
Waste of substance and man's unavailing anger —
All, all is in my web. What joy have other women
Like to this joy of a woman sovereign and laughing?
Only Athene I fear, and the bird flying left.

John Glassco

VILLANELLE I

My love and yours must be enjoyed alone:
My sleeping sister and infernal twin,
I know your body better than my own.

Only the natural conscience of the bone
Protests the sadness of the dream wherein
My love and yours must be enjoyed alone;

But the body has reasons to the soul unknown:
The soul of another is dark, said Augustine;
I know your body better than my own.

You that know everything that can be known,
Tell me through what punishment of what sin
My love and yours must be enjoyed alone?

Why have the darkness and the distance grown,
Why do we fear to let the stranger in?
— I know your body better than my own,

I know the lamp is out, the bird has flown.
To find that end where other loves begin
My love and yours must be enjoyed alone:
I know your body better than my own.

THE PLACES WHERE
THE DEAD HAVE WALKED

The places where the dead have walked
    Possess them wholly: the true tomb
Of love is in the circle chalked
By fancy where the dead have walked
    As in a visitable room,

An immense grave. What piece of ground
    Impressed by a beloved foot
But has not gathered up the sound
To keep it captive underground
    And store its music underfoot?

And so I walk continually
    Upon these paths she visited
Day after day, who is to me
The dead. Along this hollow she
    Would pass with soft and eager tread

And looks more varied than the wind,
    To watch the squirrels' hide-and-seek;
And on this hill, where time has thinned
The grasses, kneel against the wind
    To draw the daisies to her cheek.

She shall not walk this way again,
    Nor climb this hill, nor that descend,
Nor mingle in the sun and rain
With presences which now, in vain,
    Her vision and her feet attend;

That face will no more droop to lave
    With tears the daisy's pointed crown—
Never to smile within its grave
Till heaven unclose to damn and save
    And moon and stars come tumbling down!

John Glassco

And yet, to every sense but love's
   Unheard, her walking to and fro
She wakes an echo in the groves
Where my familiar sorrow moves
   And where it is compelled to go,

As if this sorrow for the guest
   Who stayed so long within my heart
Were taken over and possessed
By things that loved and knew her best —
   These powers of earth in every part

Which in their dumb insentient way
   Requited all the wealth of love
She lavished on them day by day:
These places which can better say
   What made her inmost being move.

4

VILLANELLE II

Yea, though I walk through the valley
of the shadow of death, I will fear no
evil: for thou art with me.

Alas, alas, that comfortable lie,
Religion's big one! Dear, it seems to me
God will desert us when we come to die.

Souls are His business. Will he hear the cry
Wrenched from a brainless body? No, not He.
Alas, alas, that comfortable lie

Will avail us nothing when our bodies lie
Inconscient, filthy, fighting to be free:
God will desert us when we come to die,

Give us the big cold shoulder, and deny
Everything. — *In thy last hour, call on Me!*
Alas, alas, that comfortable lie

Bubbled the Saviour too. He wondered why.
The poor enthusiast lacked the wit to see
God will desert us when we come to die,

Simply because He must. Dear, you and I,
Locked in each other's arms, come let us flee —
Alas, alas! — that comfortable lie.
God will desert us when we come to die.

———————
———————

John Glassco

THE DAY

I
The day when it will not matter
The day no longer depending on another day
When time shall have run out
When nothing will matter

(When the cloudy prime movers
Love, hope, ambition
Will have ceased to move in the light of the fact
Of the final day, when the reason for them is gone)

On that day
We shall rise on our elbows and glare around us, looking
For the abolished future
In that moment of supreme consciousness
Of unmedicinable dismay
Of absolute loneliness
Of a removal from time
A severance from substance,
When the soul, naked at last, like a bird on the ocean,
    [panting in its anguish,
Will look for its non-existent home
A place, only another place
To fill the place of the abolished future
To replace an impossible city,
Groping in the weightless void
Of the day no longer leading to another day.

The day too when we shall know
That we were only milestones on the way of those we loved
That they only climbed on our loving shoulders
To attain a paradisal view
Of something whose vision we seemed to be hindering
Some marvellous city
To which we were only a bridge
Our love a swaying but necessary means;

And that the tears to be shed for our passing
Will be succeeded by a kind of rainbow
Arching between the horizons of our lifeless head and feet —
So that our desires shall be forgiven
Our ambition excused
Our existence justified
In the light of a dumb, invisible, absurd future
Which is no longer our concern.

> Here is the man in space
> The stripped, the naked man
> Lying upon the air
> The sport of time and space
> The disinherited man
> Released to wander in air
> For an agonizing space
> In a region void of man
> In a place of beating air

Will this be the time for mercy, for the sustaining wings
Of the multitudinous cherubs, the winged loves
To fan his temples? Will the prayers of those
Who have adored him all his life assist him then?
Will any pure ingenuous secular piety
Lighten the strokes falling down and down
On his eyes and shoulders on that terrible day,
Or will he still seek in his failing mind for the impossible city?

My soul, recall those midnights in September
When the sleepy autumn winds blew, warm and amorous,
Up from the lamplit river and over us,
Thou and I — whom we must at times remember!
When walking through the night we beheld in visions
Of the sleeping city our spirit's firm repose,
Luxurious, perfect, like those flowers that close
On the bees they have first made drunken with fabulous
  [visions —

Thou who keep'st yet the divine stain of my tears
Psyche, not subject to the enervate years,
Canst thou alone now escape those terrible guardians
To roam again that ecstatic city of delights,
Madder than those who pass her superb nights
Dancing to the insane music of accordions?

>   This poor man, this dying one
>   This breathing horror
>   Oppressed and insulted
>   Filthy and hopeless
>   The mask of humanity
>   Mock of consciousness
>   Where is his city
>   What is he doing?
>   —All that he is,
>   His struggle and suffering
>   Is part of ourselves
>   Exists for us only,
>   This is the last gift
>   Of his life's meaning
>   All that he sought
>   In the marvellous city
>   Relinquished and offered
>   To us the survivors
>   As it will be
>   Ours to pass on
>   To those who have taken
>   Our hearts in their keeping
>   To those who in turn
>   Will give from their bounty,
>   Out of their horror
>   Their own desolation,
>   The infinitesimal
>   Glimpse of a beautiful blessed falsehood
>   And pray to the cherubs
>   To fan our temples.

Give yourself only to love your whole life long
Give your body, your brain, your heart to whoever may
   [choose you
Out of the multitudinous forms and faces of being
Surrender as you would to the first great wave of ocean
To the first bird threading the light blue air of April
All that surging and singing, lay your cheek against it
Open your lips to desire and the liquor of its adoration
Consider only the human music taking its way to silence
Forget the stones and scents and sounds of the fabulous city
Here in the heart of another blooms a miraculous home
Hide your proud head, renounce your ridiculous freedom
Content you to be the singing prisoner of love.

        So on that day
        That final day
        Removed from time
        Dependent on nothing
        When nothing will matter,
        You will escape
        Like a mouse in the darkness
        The dream be ended
        The city forgotten
        The shadow will touch you
        Engross you wholly,
        And soon, soon
        The day of others
        Freed of your sickness,
        Their own little day
        Serene, new born
        The day of their freedom
        Dawn quietly without you.

John Glassco

THE CROWS

The crows cry over the rosy snow

I

Habit is the greatest evil,
The folding, unfolding
Of a flower in the light, the dark,
Repetition of action
Mechanical adherence to the pattern
Of sleep and waking,
Ewige Wiederkehr des Gleichen,
As also the return to places
(Touring the battlefields
Among the crosses and poppies!)
— Why did I come to this city again?

What could we have said that year, caught
Between silence and the failure of any words,
That I could say today? And so she left
And passed beneath the arcade, passing along, her shadow
  [winking
On and off, on and off, beneath each florid arch,
The little heels clacking on the marble
In the vanished sun and dust
That is shining and blowing still
Here in the square with the naked man in the fountain
And an absence of trees.

    You find these things in any Mediterranean city,
Many things out of the past,
As also in a tired back quarter, among
Blown papers, fishheads, cabbage leaves,
The window-frames peeling and every shutter
Closed against the polluted cold,
You find the house where Paganini died.

'In questa casa
Towards evening on the 24th of May
His soul rejoined the Muses and was caught up again
In the eternal harmony of things.'

II

But here the crows cry over the rose-coloured snow —
Distant in time and place but
Lodged in the heart of feeling,
And the cry is the very feeling, the thing in itself,
Della cosa custode e dispensiere —
All that experience has become
At last enclosed in three harsh notes.
Oh the notes were always beautiful
But bare, bare till picked up by a child's rapture
And every spring thereafter
Adding riches to riches,
A cumulative feast of joy
Year upon year piled up
An echoing music and echoing emotion,
Links of an interrupted joy
Coming over the snow,
Calling out of the sky.

III

In the city of Narva, thirty years ago
Two little Baltic girls have lost their kitten,
His name is Matróssik — that is, Little Sailor Boy.
    'Matróssik, Matróssik, *kss — kss — kss* . . . '
Through the streets they are crying,
Up the cobbled way to the Petriplatz,
Down by the river and past the castle of Ivan
And on and on, vainly, the sound of their voices
                dying, rising, dying, *kss — kss — kss* . . .
    And still those little girls propelled their cry

On my mind's dusty streets, year after year
In some disguise or another, long, long
Occluding my heartbeat ... Foolish, foolish
Such memories and such pathos, immoderate, suspect,
Whispers of falsity and flight —
                              And hence
By sweet and facile stages came
The retreat into erotic reverie,
The dream of Arthur,
That dark Avilion where there is no death,
Only immortal pleasure in a suspension of time
As conscience drops into the timelessness
Where the unconscious lives
Snug in its cortical layer:
                         draw back, draw in,
Enter this paradise which is always waiting
For the magician of the self, his royal visit
To a world of adoring shadows
Where lust is the only living thing,
Absolute power and absolute submission
Locked in each other's loving arms
In the darkest room of the tallest house
Where home has become a hiding-place
And communication gibberish.

      In questa casa
      The soul is sighing
      This is the school
      For the art of dying
      This is the house
      Where nothing happens.

IV

The crows are crying over the rosy snow!
Ice melts at the end of the pine-needles,
Each feathery plume a spray
An island of bright water at the branch's tip
Each needle a lustre, a thread of living water,
Each plume a little gushing spring, the whole tree
Nothing but silver, all lustre, all a wave
All watery foaming flight —
      'Awake, awake, my heart, to be loved!'
This is the same old story
The knife's ecstatic entrance into the heart
And the heart's gift of blood to the moving air.
      Awake, awake!
Gone are the partings and the wounds
All the words of farewell have returned to silence
All the shadows under the arches to darkness
And the habit and refrain of memory
Tumbles into the void like a stale provincial motto.

> This is the house
> The crows have opened
> The apple garden
> The dream of Arthur,
> Out of the sky-wrack
> The light is shed,
> Out of the silence
> The notes are coming.

John Glassco

A POINT OF SKY

Boredom, disaster and distress
Make the same furrows in the face,
The affections find a common line
Between mouth and eyebrow: the mirror
Has told you so. And today, in prison,
You are sad with the weight of a moment
Suddenly descended, simply to remember
What you were, reflect on what you are,
On time's reverses, and what brought you here
(Which is anywhere: this room and mountain, this rainy day)
To a kind of stopping-place, a centre
In the midst of a maze, and what makes you pause
And stare into the quiet rain
With all its millions of descending points,
Into all that fluency from this point of rest.
      So it happens, from time to time,
The suspended sentence falling on us like a fist,
The shape of blackness into which we are always moving:
Not the sudden, shattering terror
With something of the divine in it, which is
A certain contact and connection with God,
But the descent of the terrible clarity of tedium,
The vision of the true face of our condition,
The man in the mirror who is always there.

          A house is falling
          A dog is dying
          A bird is singing
          A woman is crying
          A window is open
          But air will not enter
          There is no communion
          Of settling and death
          Of song and sorrow

Only the whirring
Of weights in a circle
A winking of lights
A passage of bodies
A cry in the darkness
As the world turns over

And you thought there would always be time,
Occasions to seize the occasion, combine the elements
Dazzle your own eyes with the work,
But there is no time;
In this hour the future has suddenly shrunken
Into the compass of the catoptric past,
Caught and pinned in a single glance
In this moment of inalterable vision,
Of sense and hearing sharpened to an agonized awareness
Of the tick of time when there is no time,
Of the pulse of life when life has been abolished.
You thought there would always be time
To arrange matters, to set the metals in order.
You thought there would always be life
And now there is only the flaming circle
Moving in aimless waves,
A dis·urbance of fire troubling the stillness.
    Was there ever time? And the question raises
The question of a possible excuse
For what was left undone, the turning not taken,
The hardness not embraced, for the choice of a meadow
Drowsing in a white light of happiness,
A choice of the gate into that meadow and that light
Rather than the dark road ascending
Between the violet buildings, up and up
Towards an infinitesimal point of sky.
Who is to say there was never time nor occasion?
Only the demon who stands behind the shoulder,
The dark one, the unanswerable,

Who knows best, who is always right,
The master of salutary denials.
— No, there was never a choice
Of a turning towards the hard blue point of sky!
For even the future is only in the present,
Its hopes and terrors are here and now
And our pleasure and our death
Are consummated every day:
We are already happy
We are already dying
In the moment of speculation
Which holds the shape of the beauty and terror of the
    [experience,
The haze and the storm,
In the moment which holds all our knowledge
As the poise and strain of pleasure is held in the
    [beloved's mouth,
As her glance in the morning of meeting
Holds the whole history of our passion
Multiplying and making rich the events
That will never arrive.

        In this moment
        Of rest, this halting
        Of hope and memory
        Of all things falling
        Away from the body,
        Of a drift of silence
        Upon all feeling,
        With the rain falling
        Between the spaces
        Upon the vision
        Of all things, halting
        The mind's motion
        Stopping the springs,
        Think of the refuge,

The point of sky,
The certain castle,
The certain presence
Behind the appearance shaling, shaling
In pieces and powder.

Press with both hands the walls on either side
Bear up against the dark and descending vault
For the meadow has vanished and the point of sky also
Memory alone has built them into your mind
With their essence caught in the odour of clover
And in the sound of a clean blue wind blowing—
They are only the last of the inviolacies
You take with you into this little room
The prison and refuge of your life's remains.
Strive with both hands against the encroaching dark
Blow with your breath against the eructations
Deny, always deny that you are diminishing
Let your words burst like blisters in the face of the law
Asserting always it was not made for you.
Stop your ears against the beloved and sickly intimations
The slurred passage of slippered feet passing your door
Only to pass, never to pause
To pass on to a further door
Leading away to landings, stairs
And passages past other doors
Those tired restless feet never to halt
To be followed by no knocking
No visitation or communication
Only passing along and away—
Fight with both hands against the prison of God
And against the prison of time and eternal power
Let not your hands fail nor your desperation weaken
Against the warders who have shut the sky against you

That my regrets
May so shine before me

All the hours of my life
That I shall not sleep, and my eyes open
That I shall not die, and my heart beating
But shall remember always
The point of sky and the meadow
The thing foregone and the thing achieved
So that the beauty of both is united
In one clear flame of longing.

ONE LAST WORD

For M. McC.

Now that I have your hand, let me persuade you
The means are more important than the end,
Ends being only an excuse for action,
For adventures sought for their own sake alone,
Pictures along the way, feelings
Released in love: so, acting out our dreams
We justify movement by giving it a purpose
(Who can be still forever?)
This is the rationale of travel
And the formula of lovers.

Dearest, it is not for the amusement of certain tissues,
Nor for whatever may thread our loins like a vein
                              of miraculous water
That now (under the music) I speak your name—
But for the journey we shall take together
Through a transfigured landscape
Of beasts and birds and people
Where everything is new.
                         Listen,
The embarkation for Cythera[10]
Is eternal because it ends nowhere:
No port for those tasselled sails! And for our love
No outcome,
Only the modesty
The perfection
Of the flight or death of a bird.

———————————
——————————————
———————————

5

from MONMONTREAL[11]

[Part I]

Last night, on the final stroke of four, when I awoke
To the snowbound city of my dead childhood, the dead stroke
Of the final silence when the streets pause to take breath
In a respite of their mad progression towards death —
Dumb city, lashed back into a recreated youth
Of rectangular steel, a metal mask upon your mouth,
Last night I heard again all your chanting voices
Fetched from my own dead childhood, and all the noises
Of the bells, the bells of churches, horses and the tramways
Ringing and groaning on the rails of all the damned ways
Memory constructs out of the age it passed alone
In a house of muted winter — yes, then my very own
Your silence, your ruin, your ravishment, your pride:
On that sad bellstroke they were all mine, and my spirit died
In a smokeless whiff of unpretending rage
In a rented room between Crescent Street and Côte des Neiges.

[from Part V]

O childhood streets of Montreal
Simpson where I was born
St. Luke where I was terrified
Mackay where I went to school
Crescent and Bishop where I played in a
    [tasselled tuque
On your iron-railed grey-stone steps,

There are some winding garbage-littered lanes
Behind you still, and lately, in the spring
I have retraced those corners where I lived and died
So many times; where my mouth was stuffed with sooty snow;

97

Where I loved a little girl in pantalettes
Whose last name I have forgotten—
And like a wandering dog staking some lost terrain
Urinated willy-nilly in the dust, looking
Cautiously upwards,
Down and around.

---

from SQUIRE HARDMAN[12]

And so the touzle-headed lad appears,
Clad in a nightgown that befits his years,
A garment brief and simple, and well-plann'd
For execution of the work in hand;
And see, by Jove, the cunning little sweep
This very moment has begun to weep,
As if he felt his skin already smart
And hop'd his tears might soften *Mary's* heart:
Vain hope, my luckless Tom, and vain those tears:
Your b-m's account is too much *in arrears*!

Now *Mary* smiles and speaks him tenderly,
Bids him approach and takes him on her knee,
And fondling him with motherly affection,
Informs him that his temper needs correction,
And the bad habits into which he's slipping
Must be arrested by a nice warm whipping;
Whilst, as she speaks, the cowering urchin's eye
Is fixed upon the table standing by,
Where lies, all ready coil'd, the supple strap
Whose sting he knows full well, poor little chap!
And I in turn survey the pleasing scene
In expectation silent and serene,

So when the lecture rounds unto its close
My spirits are at the proper height, God knows.

      But now tis time the real game began,
The sport that warms the English gentleman
To amorous play, — and in a twinkling, see
How Tom is stretched across my good right knee,
His trembling legs close gripp'd between my thighs,
His hands secur'd in mine as in a vise:
When *Mary* whisks his shirt up to his waist,
How more expertly could a boy be plac'd?
I smile to see her raise the strap, for who
Has now a better vantage-point and view
O' th' *spheres of operation* than I do?
And when the thong with an impetuous hiss
Begins to fall, who can describe my bliss?
I mark each rosy welt the leather makes,
I see the chubby flesh that shrinks and shakes,
I hear the screams and sobs, the desp'rate pleas,
And feel each bound and struggle twixt my knees;
While as th' unhappy urchin leaps and squirms,
My *Mary* lectures him in formal terms,
And with a store of comfortable saws
Improves each moment when she makes a pause.

John Glassco

JANUARY

by Louis Fréchette (1839–1908)

The storm has ceased. The keen and limpid air
Has spread a silver carpet on the stream
Where, on intrepid leg, the skater glides
With shimmering flame upon his iron shoe.

Far from her warm boudoir, a lady braves
Beneath her bearskin robes the biting air;
With a sound of golden bells her rapid sleigh
Flashes like lightning past our dazzled eyes.

And later, through the nights' ideal cold
While thousands of auroras in the sky
Flutter their plumage like fantastic birds,

In ambered salons — deity's new shrines —
T'orchestral strains, 'neath sparkling chandeliers,
The gay quadrille unreels its sinuous web!

THE *TERROIR*

(The three following poems are sufficient to show the complexion of the 'poetry of the land', so famous in its own day and now so properly forgotten.)

THE PLOUGHMAN

by William Chapman (1850–1917)

Behind two oxen or plodding Percherons
The man walks bent in the lonely field; his hand
Is riveted to the handle of the plough.
He is opening up the belly of the land.

Sunlight floods the base of the green hill;
The darling soil receives his fixèd stare:
Drunk with the heavy scent the fallow breathes,
He lines his furrows with deliberate care.

And, musing, sometimes he will sketch a smile. ˙
His ear already seems to hear suspire
A sea of gold under a sun of fire;

He sees the harvest in his barn bestowed;
He dreams that an angel counts his steps the while,
And knows the ploughman shares the work of God.

———————
———————

THE HAUNTED HOUSE

by Nérée Beauchemin (1850–1931)

It heaves its gable under the grizzled moss,
And the great dormer, edged with wooden lace,
Is a kind of frame for the shattered window whence
I used to watch the splendid evenings pass.

Crying in the wind, the door has fallen open.
Caught in the trap of memory, I see
A faint light flickering from the blackened chimney
On icy ceilings and an empty hall.

On the sloping roof there is a shadow, leaning
In the window-frame. . . . The unseen evenings die;
The soul of a house so often cloaked in mourning,
Wrapped in its sadness, gazes at the sky.

MIDDAY IN THE FIELDS

by Gonsalve Desaulniers (1863–1934)

Noon. From the steeple of the parish church has pealed
The Angelus. The reapers drive the team
Under the birch-trees bordering the green field,
And fall to sharpening their scythes whose edges gleam
Under the day's hot kiss. Where the hay is piled
In stacks, the mother (modestly withdrawn)
Offers a milk-swollen breast to her newborn child,
And smiles — while under the Heaven's wide profound
Whose sleepy peace only the bells break in upon,
Her man has crossed himself, without a sound.

IMPRESSIONS OF SNOW AND FROST

by Albert Lozeau (1878–1924)

I

The trees are like white statues growing
Out of white sidewalks and by white rooftops swirled
With a foam of heavenly whiteness: Look, it is snowing!
Snowing as if the clouds had broken against the
   [wind and curled
Backward and were all falling in thousands of
   [snowflakes and all going
To cover the black earth of this old and sinful world.
The fields, where the snow has all day long been falling,
Look from here like a lake of curdled milk; a trine
Of silvery bells on the roads where the snow is balling
Tinkles an instant in the wind's cold whine;
And the little children are calling out gaily, calling
For joy of the sky's white powder upon this land of mine.

II

A snowflake melts in a tear upon my window.
I close my book in the middle of a page
To watch the snow out of the white sky falling
And follow its slow and spiralling pilgrimage.
It is soft and alive, fantastical and doting,
Gliding and floating, eddying and flying,
Now gay, now grave, like a poet versifying
Who follows the wild vagaries of his whim,
As either a little listless wind comes blowing
Or a new breath all of a sudden keeps it going!
Yet all this ends, for the snowflake and for him,
In a long fit of weeping and in water flowing ...

III

Today, my window is nothing but white leaves
Frozen in blanchèd tremors on the glass,
Frost-flowers, fruits of rime and silver sheaves;
Trees made of silver-gilt, entwined together,
Seem to be waiting for a wind to pass,
Quiet and soft and white. Calm little frame!
Where in the drowned repose of sleeping water
This garden lies insensible as in death,
Your scene will melt in the warmth of the first flame
Like the pure dreams our youthful spirit lost,
And all the hopes and illusions mourned below our breath:
On the heart's window, fragile flowers of frost . . .

IV

In these long winter evenings when the eyes,
Wearied of books, fix on the window-pane
Where the frost draws, with slow mysterious pen,
Under the influence of the raging wind,
In gardens and woods forever white and calm
The marvellous flower and the fantastic palm —
These evenings, in his solitary room,
Comparing the darkness lurking in his mind
With the white splendour of the things of night,
The poet, isolated from mankind,
Thinks of the grand peace of December's tombs,
And of their ermine shrouds, so noiselessly
Heaped up and shining under the moonlit sky.

6

Three Notes on the Poetic Process

THE OPAQUE MEDIUM[13]

Remarks on the Translation of Poetry with a Special Reference to French-Canadian Verse

The translation of poetry is often decried. It has become fashionable to repeat Robert Frost's remark that what gets lost in the process is "the poetry itself" — or, as Sir John Denham put it rather less succintly three hundred years earlier, "the subtile Spirit of poesie evaporates entirely in the transfusion from one language to another", though he added the saving qualification, "unless a new, or an original spirit is infused by the Translator himself". This infusion remains the mark of good translation; and difficult as it is, the operation must always be ruled by the architecture of the poem itself, which is necessarily laid bare. Faithful translation especially, which can seldom hope — and in the opinion of some should never try — to reproduce the music or magic of the original, is in fact the strictest examination which a poem's intimate structure can undergo, an ultimate screening which may leave it nothing but its intellectual content or "meaning", its images and inner pulsation; for Mallarmé's clever riposte to Degas is only half true: poetry *is* made out of words, but poems themselves — as Mallarmé must have known — do not *begin* with words but with ideas, moods, concepts, formulations of emotion. The scales of translation are thus weighted in favour of a poetry marked by clarity of thought and expression, spare and striking imagery, and a simple internal movement: the work of Virgil, Dante, Villon and Baudelaire — to take four examples at random — lends itself admirably to versions in other tongues; while that of Catullus, Tasso, Hugo and Verlaine does not; Rimbaud's richly allusive prose-poems are almost unreadable in translation, though his sonnets and "ballads", due to their comparative simplicity, come through quite well.

107

But it is not only the ideas and progression of a poem which are exposed by translation: the temper and complexion of the poet himself are so mercilessly revealed as to justify the wry old equation of *traduttore, traditore.* This betrayal, which is part of the translator's enforced role of analytical critic, is inevitable. For the good translator is obliged, whether he like it or not, either to take the line laid down by Lord Roscommon in that ingenuous couplet,

> *Your author always will the best advise;*
> *Fall when he falls, and when he rises rise,*

or yield to the temptation to beautify and "improve", and thus perhaps carry the process of betrayal still further.

Why then, it may be asked, make translations of poetry at all? If the result is a loss, a depreciation, a betrayal, surely the expense of effort, the dizzying labour of trying to transmute the essence of that most incommensurable thing, a poem, might be better applied elsewhere — even in following Ezra Pound's advice to "make it new", that is, to misread the text in a fit of inspired illiteracy and make another poem altogether. But is not this question only another and insidious way of asking why poetry itself should be written? The poet, as Saint-Denys-Garneau found, is aware sooner or later that in pursuing his vocation he is exposing, depreciating and betraying himself, and finally failing to express the reality of his experience; but this does not stop him from writing poetry. In the same way, the devoted translator of poetry will not be balked: he is possessed by the necessity of making a *translation* — in the older, religious sense of a conveyance or assumption, as of Enoch or Elijah — of the vision of reality he has received from a poem, and of communicating his experience to those of another tongue; and when he wholly succeeds, as he sometimes does, the sense of achievement is that of poetic creation itself. At the worst, he has made a bridge of sorts.

The history of serious translation of French Canadian poetry is short, covering little more than a dozen years and comprising only the collections of Jean Beaupré and Gael Turnbull (1955), G.R. Roy (1958), P.F. Widdows (1960), F.R. Scott (1964) and Peter Miller (1964), although isolated groups of poems have appeared from time to time in books, newspapers and the little magazines; and almost all the chosen poets date from within the last twenty-five years. Of translations done before 1950 there is little worth preserving except for antiquarian reasons — some of the happy exceptions being the work in the thirties of Regina Shoolman, A.M. Klein, W.R. Eadie and Grace Davignon. Going further back, one has only to read the translations done around the turn of the century, with their faded prettiness, poetic diction and Victorian tinkle, to appreciate the new, profound and sensitive treatment accorded the poetry of French Canada within the last five years.

The leading figure in this field so recently opened up is undoubtedly F.R. Scott, whose early renderings of Garneau, Hébert, Hénault, Trottier, Pilon and Giguère are still outstanding, his taste, fidelity and grasp of the movement of each poem are always admirable, and his versions could serve as models: he is Canada's first artistic translator of poetry — and his recent versions of young poets like Fernand Ouellette and Jacques Brault show that his hand has lost none of its cunning. The joint work of Beaupré and Turnbull — whose little mimeographed pamphlets, produced in Iroquois Falls in 1955–1956, are now collectors' items — has in spite of all its faults a place of honour as the first example of collective poetry translation in this country; Roy's miscellany is noteworthy as an example of poetry translation at its weakest; while Widdows and Miller, in their selections from the work of Nelligan and Grandbois respectively, have given English readers a glimpse, at least, of two important poets of French Canada. In the last two years, however, the translation of French-Canadian poetry has been immeasurably enriched by the work of such outstanding English-Canadian poets as G.V. Downes, Louis Dudek, R.A.D. Ford, Eldon Grier, Ralph Gustafson, George Johnston, Jay Macpherson, James Reaney, A.J.M. Smith and Francis Sparshott.[1]

This recent access of fine new work may be taken as a hopeful sign for the future. On the other hand, the growing enthusiasm for translating French Canadian poetry has brought certain problems in its train.

---

[1] A comprehensive collection of the best of all this work, presenting French-Canadian poetry from Crémazie to the present day and comprising more than 200 poems, has been edited by the present writer and will appear in the spring under the imprint of Oxford University Press (Toronto). [The work in question, *The Poetry of French Canada in Translation*, was published in 1970.]

The translation of poetry is one of the most difficult and exacting literary disciplines. Every poet knows it is easier to write a poem than to translate one: his task is here one of veritable re-creation, and is moreover made harder and more discouraging by the virtual impossibility — except in very rare cases — of at once doing justice to the original and remaining faithful to it, and by the constant necessity of choosing between the two challenges of fidelity and true poetry. The translator must therefore not only thoroughly understand the language of his original text, as well as be familiar with the whole body of its literature, but he must also be a good poet himself. If only one of these conditions is met, the result will be an exercise in either graceless pedantry or laughable misunderstanding, and where both are lacking we will have, alas, such absurdities as the rendering of this line of Grandbois,

> *Une extraordinaire ivresse coulait le long*
> *de mes frissons et mes pas imaginaient la*
> *mesure d'une immobilité fatalement dérisoire*[2]

> An extraordinary intoxication ran the length
> of my shivers and my steps imagined the
> measure of a fatally derisive immobility;

or these lines of André Major

> *je parle d'une terre froide à nourrir de brûlures*
> *je parle pour qui passe innocent dans la machine à épuisement*[3]

as

> I speak about a cold country in which to nourish burns
> I speak for one who passed them by without knowing in his
> [worn-out tricks;

or these of Gaston Miron,

> *Et je m'écris sous la loi d'émeute*
> *je veux saigner sur vous pour toute l'affection*[4]

---

[2] From *Ah, toutes ces rues . . .* , in *les Iles de la Nuit* (1944).
[3] From *Verte ma parole*, in *le Pays* (1963).
[4] From *l'Homme agonique*, uncollected.

as

> And of me I write in riot's grip
> wanting by every affected place to bleed on you;

or even these of Anne Hébert,

> *L'allée de pins*
> *Se ravine*
> *Comme un mauvais chemin*[5]

as

> The alley of pines
> Yawns open
> Like a bad road;

all of which, and countless others equally ridiculous, have appeared in reputable anglophone literary magazines within the last two years, and several in publicly subsidized books.

It is regrettable that such displays of ignorance and laziness are multiplying faster than good translations — though it is only natural they should, since they demand so little time or effort. But it is also dangerous; for there is a law, corresponding to Gresham's, by which bad translation smothers and drives out good, the translatee becoming in a sense the property of his first translator, for better or worse, and bad translations acquiring a kind of squatters' rights in the eyes of both reader and publisher.

The remedy is of course in the poet's own hands: he can refuse to allow a bad translation to be printed. But he is often unable to judge; and in almost all cases the temptation of seeing his work in another language will outweigh all other considerations. The situation is further confused by the fact that many translations of French-Canadian poems are now being printed without their authors' permission or even knowledge.

It may be argued that these are, after all, only small clouds in the sky, that any interest in the riches of French-Canadian poetry, now enjoying the most important revolution and renascence in its history, must be welcomed, and that even the worst translation cannot

---

[5] From *Vieille image*, in *le Tombeau des rois* (1953).

wholly spoil its original, since something of the emotion, the images, the pulse and internal movement, always comes through, as in a palimpsest. But this is really fair neither to the public nor the original poet.

The poetry of French Canada should not be presented to its wide and growing anglophone audience in the form of travesty if it continues to be so, thus evoking merely puzzlement, disdain or laughter — and goodness knows the above examples can evoke nothing else — no good will have been served. The peculiar genius, delicacy and insight of French-Canadian poetry will have been hopelessly stultified and misrepresented, and the wretched *traduttore-traditore* equation confirmed. The only remedy rests with the subsidizing bodies, which must be persuaded that the translation of poetry calls for linguistic competence, taste and poetic ability, and that nothing less than this will do.

EUTERPE'S HONEYMOON:[14]

Notes on the Poetic Process

As an ex-poet (for the Muse, alas, deserted me about three years ago) I feel I can now declare my belief that ideas are of little importance in the "purest" kind of poetry, i.e., the finished song or lyric. Such poetry can, I propose, do very well without any idea or intellectual content at all.

There is really nothing new in this proposition, but readers of poetry may be interested to know that while the lyric poem can get along very well without ideas, the poet himself, while he is composing it, is not so lucky; for the idea he is expressing must be, even when not clearly grasped, of supreme intellectual importance to *him*—unless of course he is merely poeticizing, that is, writing a *chose vecue*, or emitting an orgasmic or agonized yelp, or doing a landscape, or—like so many poets on the West Coast—playing "Indian". What I mean is that the poet must be wholly possessed by the rationale of his poem but that, paradoxically, this rationale is of little importance to the poem itself; if it is conveyed, confusedly or even minimally, that is enough. What is important is the passion it arouses in the poet's mind. The poet's mind, not the reader's. (At this point the reader is of no importance.) This passion is of almost limitless variety: it can be love, despair, hope, fear, awe, horror, disgust, melancholy, compassion; but it is as the expression of one or other of such emotions that the poem itself exists. It then becomes the poem's whole business to convey one or even several of these emotions—not the intellectual idea or moral judgment or philosophical truth with which it started in the poet's mind. (Good poems do not begin in an undisciplined welter of emotion.) Here is where the emotion takes over, initiating the second stage of composition. My own practice (for whatever it was worth) was, whenever in the course of writing a poem I found the idea conflicting with the emotion, to put the idea in second place—occasionally even to clear it right out of the poem, as a house-painter does with his scaffolding once the job is finished.

And this brings us to the crucial question: what are the elements of a good poem? (We are thinking now of the reader.) I have already proposed that its intellectual content is of little or no importance

113

compared to its emotional force and impact. But we must go a little further than this.

I was once asked at a literary party, by an academic person, what must a poem *have* to be a good poem? I said, extempore, that all I could see was that it must have a beginning, a middle and an end. He replied that Aristotle had said the same thing some time ago, at which point there was some kind of drunken interruption and the discussion was broken off. But the question, and my own unrehearsed answer, set up a train of thought whose conclusions may now be submitted in a more extended and coherent form.

It seems to me, then that the main *technical* (if one may so call it) element of a successful lyric poem is its *internal movement*, since this is what really determines the form. The emotion may be any of those I mentioned earlier; the outer form or casing may be anything at all, from acrostical sestina to little cement blocks of concrete verse. But it must above all be so constructed that it has a single major and continuous pulsation. Without this vital and vivifying element, the poem will fall apart and fail.

Now then, is it possible actually to chart this essential pulsating movement of a good lyric? Not the beauty or illumination of any one line or sequence of lines, but the entire course or progression of its thought and even, if possible, the generally parallel course of the constantly deepening delight it gives? If so, this course will I think be found to consist of a series of forward and backward movements, of alternating thrusts and retreats, or advancements and withdrawals, but with each term related to the other more as a kind of pause than an actual gain or loss of illumination, as something like a rest in music. It is surely no coincidence that the nature of this progression of delight is similar to that of the ecstatic process of composition itself which, as beautifully described by Coleridge, resembles the progress of the water-beetle against the stream, a succession of alternate spells of swimming and resting. (Every good poem is re-composed by the good reader, and often improvised.) But the final progression of the finished poem is of course more complex, varied and uneven than the process of its composition, and would seem at first glance to be obeying its own peculiar and mysterious law. Yet this law, though applied with the poet's own individual instinct for rightness, may be found, I think, to be laid down by some larger collective authority which stands outside and above both poet and poem, and while the behests of this authority (let us call it the Muse) have not been codified or reduced to any order (no, not even by the critical acumen of Northrop Frye—whom, by the way, all *young* poets should avoid reading), I see no reason to believe they do not exist, as a kind of imprecise but constant fiat of man's aesthetic sensibility. Observe my concern for order, that last infirmity of a poetic-disorderly mind.

It has been suggested that our appreciation of music, for example that of Bach, has nothing to do with sound. John Hoyle tells us that "what we appreciate, through music, in the brain are electrical signals that we receive from the ears," that "our use of sound is simply a convenient device for generating certain patterns of electrical activity," and that it is possible that "musical rhythms reflect the main electrical rhythms that occur in the brain." If there is any substance in this theory, it is likely that the progression of a lyric poem, in both the poet and the reader, reflects a similar set of electrical rhythms. (The exquisite 'natural' balance between octave and sestet in a sonnet comes to mind: how else could the form have survived for over seven hundred years?)

Disturbing as this might at first appear to writers and readers of lyric poetry, we should not forget that the progression of a poem is a purely technical element of its make-up and, while important, is only an adjunct, a kind of of tool by which idea and emotion—those deeper and more mysterious elements—may be presented with greater clearness, cogency and beauty.

So we come back, inevitably, to the question of "inspiration", of the Muses, the sacred Nine—especially to Euterpe who presides over the lyric poem. A lovely teaser, this one, always kissing you and running away. Irving Layton's notion of her absolute *possession* of him is attractive but, like all his ideas, simplistic and vaguely suspect. I think he is apparently downgrading himself merely to confuse his *bêtes noires* the critics: "Look, you eunuchs, I know this girl, see? And you don't." And he does indeed. But we all do, we writers and readers of poetry, and so, even though to a sadly limited extent, must the dusty and over-decried academics themselves—though surely not as the besotted partners of some White Goddess *anima mundi* or praying mantis (the epithets are D.G. Jones') who captures and then discards us.

For poetic creation—like poetic appreciation—is not simply a possession, a kind of mindless swoon: it is rather, I think, like an old-fashioned "happy" marriage of the natural and supernatural, a short sweet honeymoon of Poet and Muse. Valery's fifty-fifty proportion of their share in the work—one line of the alexandrine from her, and the other rhyming one from him—seems a pretty fair assessment of the joint authorship of a lyric poem. (Baudelaire, I admit, tells us that about eighty per cent of a poem is a clever, laborious process of "faking"—though like Poe he may have been showing off a little.) But it is the poet who decides on the final version, and in this decision his conscious intellect, his taste, plays an agonizing part: because this is when he receives Euterpe's faint, final, fleeting orders: *do it this way, you dope: don't ask me why*—and he can never be sure if anyone else will understand. The best thing is to go along with Euterpe: she may not know what she's talking about, but she's talking about what she knows.

And the worst things is for the poet to let himself be seduced, either by the lures of sensationalism or virtuosity, into indulging in facile surprises or charming sonorities. The poetic honeymoon will then become an absurd and horrible adventure, with the maladroit poet sweating alone in the temple bedroom and Euterpe locking herself in the bathroom to weep: *how could he do this to me?* I can think of many such honeymoons in our poetry.[15]

THE POET AS PERFORMER DEBASES HIS ART

You hear him, not his poetry.[16]

At the annual meeting of the League of Canadian Poets last May, it was reported that exactly 100 poetry recitations had been given by its members during 1976; they were held in universities, libraries, parish halls and high school auditoriums all across Canada, and were of course funded by the Canada Council. Since the League now numbers 160 members—and due to the present tidal wave of poetic genius in Canada they are constantly growing—it is clear that the practice and encouragement of poets reading their work in public is reaching epidemic proportions.

Back in the Sixties these recitations seemed no more than amusing novelty, a passing fad, a concession to the illiterate, not to be taken seriously. Who can forget the coffee-house poet of those days, in his uniform of jeans, work-shirt, beard and granny glasses, reading—interminably and in an almost inaudible monotone—his almost incomprehensible verses? A figure of fun, you would have said. But since then, due partly to efficient and tireless promotion by the League, the figure has grown larger, cast a longer shadow, growing canny as it caught on to what its audience wanted; it learned to simplify its message, to enunciate clearly, use a microphone, vary its voice, employ gestures, play to the gallery and make its hearers laugh. Soon, and almost insensibly, the poet had become a performer.

This was already apparent at the first mammoth 20-poet recital staged by the League in 1968. The serious poets, with their straightforward, dignified and dull delivery, made little impression. It was the showmen who stole the show. They delivered non poems, often little more than wordless chants or humorous monologues; but these were given with such skill and brio that the horse-laughs of applause were loud and spontaneous. Exercises in mindless diatribe were even more successful, and I recall one of these which repeatedly adjured the listener to screw a long list of institutions, attitudes and people. It was the sensation of the evening, drawing shrieks and whistles of approval.

Since then, this appreciation of voiced poetry has reached the further level reported by Anne Marriott, a well-known poet now

117

teaching creative writing in Vancouver: "I have seen students from Grade 3 to third-year university respond overwhelmingly to a b.p. nichol chant: each student chanting the name of a vegetable in a round, like 'row your boat' until the whole room is rocking with sound — gets to the oral beginnings of poetry and makes a real good noise."

This kind of total participation, while probably harmless for young children, is surely neither healthy nor desirable for the average university student, who is both highly susceptible and already semi-literate. Indeed, as Northrop Frye declares, "a 'real' or fully engaged response to art does not heighten consciousness but lowers and debases it."

But it is not too difficult to trace the rationale of such a response. It stems, I should say, from the naive listener's belief that he is getting "closer" to a poem by hearing it from the poet himself. This belief seems to be on a par with the feelings of the person who believes he is getting closer, say, to the spirit of Joyce's *Ulysses* by wandering around Dublin. The truth is exactly the opposite: such "closeness" actually hinders his appreciation of the text by adulterating it with an easy, tempting and impertinent emotion. And with a living, breathing, mouthing poet facing one on a public stage, the adulteration is still greater, for not only is one listening to *him* more than to what he is saying but, as part of a crowd, one is not so much having an esthetic experience as participating in a communal one.

It is very doubtful if the interests of poetry are being served by making it a social event at all. Poetry, at any rate as we now know it, is best received in a state of isolation and tranquility, through the printed page. Moreover, for such reception, the eye is vastly superior to the ear; moving faster than the voice and serving the intelligence more directly, it can also take in at a preliminary glance the shape and length of a poem, so that the mind is prepared, as it were, for the degree and kind of attention it will be called on to give; it can also re-read and meditate a difficult or obscure passage; and finally, it can master the poem's verbal music much better, for there is no doubt that the educated *inward* ear can do more with the rhythms, vowels, syncopations and stresses of any poem than the amateur human voice can hope to do.

But there is a further reason to look askance at these recitations. For the poet who recites cannot help noting that his lighter, chattier, funnier and "sexier" poems receive the most applause from his audience, and unless he is a very strong character — which most poets are not — he may find himself composing this kind of *vers de société* rather than serious verse.

I cannot of course deny there is a great deal of a certain kind of pleasure to be had from hearing poetry well recited. The irony is that so often we discover, on reading the poem later for ourselves, it was a bad poem; we had been seduced by the beauty of its voicing, the grace and expertise of its delivery, the personality of the poet himself. Whether that pleasure was "true" is a matter for the metaphysicians. Like the pleasure of one of those young men of medieval stories who enjoys, in pitch darkness, the favors of a hideous crone while believing she is the beautiful maiden he loves, ours was, I suppose, none the less true for being founded on a similar misapprehension. But the situation in reverse is unfortunately just as true, for we all know how badly good poets can voice their best poems; only call to mind the liturgical drone of Eliot, the metronomic drought of Stevens, the frothy rant of Thomas, the breathy melodrama of Pound, all painfully immortalized on recordings; these are things we must forget.

And this raises the whole question of the poet's role in society. Should he be a performer at all? The Montreal poet Sharon Nelson has argued that "to suggest that poets submit themselves to the disciplined work on their bodies and voices which an actor does is like telling a playwright that he may not create a character he cannot, or would not, act." She then sums up the problem stating, "The job of a poet is to write poetry. The 'poetry business' — all those auxiliary activities which allow poets to get ahead, to secure jobs as writers in residence, make a little money and seduce an audience — do little to encourage fine writing."

In any case, and for better or worse, we are still in the typographic era, and our final judgments should be literate rather than audiovisual, and arrived at privately rather than *en masse*. As Nelson wryly reminds us, "Oral tradition continues to thrive among illiterate peoples," and it is a little disturbing to see its recrudescence among us now, as in the bacchanalia in Toronto a year ago at the three-day International Poetry Festival in Hart House when, according to *The Montreal Gazette*, "at the poetry reading marathon on closing night, wine, mime, lyrics, chanting, dance, howling, gurgling, touching and exploding all wove the performance and the audience together into a heightened form of life-poetic consciousness."

Such excesses, though probably self-corrective, do underline the direction that poetry recitations may well be taking: that is, toward the idea of poetry as a mindless emotional release, a kind of pentecostal "service of witness" — with the poet as priest or shaman — or, what is almost as bad, simply as pseudo-cultural vaudeville, a form of "showbiz".

NOTES

NOTES

1. THE WHITE MANSION was a large country house that Glassco and his friend and companion, Graeme Taylor, had acquired some time in 1936/37, and which Glassco described as "A 16-room house with 5 bathrooms and acres of grounds" (letter of February 5, 1941 to Robert McAlmon). It was situated a short distance outside the village of Knowlton in Québec's Eastern Townships, and was, reputedly, the scene of some fast and wild living, which included a *ménage-à-trois* with a woman referred to as Sappho, who later—August 1942—became Graeme Taylor's wife.
2. Lyaeus, also Dionysus, in Greek mythology the son of Zeus and Semele, and appearing here in his role as a god of wine who loosens care and inspires to music and poetry.
3. Originally published in *Delta* (Canada), No. 21 (May 1963), the poem was dedicated to Olivier Messaien (b. 1908), a French composer and organist who is noted for his unusual theories of composition based on scales of his own invention and on birdsong. Glassco's poem appeared with the following notation on its onomatopeia which may very well bespeak a certain kind of tongue-in-cheekiness:

   > In explanation of the poem facing this page, John Glassco writes: "Beginning with the note of the orchard oriole, it rises at once to the almost Shelleyan ecstasy of Wilson's Thrush, then assumes in succession the twinkling, sportive character of the common song-sparrow and the tedious garrulity of the house wren, becoming by swift gradations fanciful, humorous, satirical, familiar and at last descending to the rather jejune coarseness of line 12 and culminating in the two harsh notes ('Craow! 'tsh-aow!') which are probably the bird's only original form of expression. This, however, is soon followed by the two deep philosophical notes of the flicker ('Queah? Pueah!'), and succeeded, after a short tune-up, by the wonderfully sustained amorous pathos of the line 'kooka prea, etc.' based on (though infinitely superior to) the song of the robin. This whole line is extremely beautiful. Then, for no apparent reason, the bird breaks out in two loud squawks of anger, and almost at once falls into a soft, sweet tone of self-pity, communing with itself in the murmur ending in the delicate 'tshippewat 'wurr-wurr'. After the heart-rending despair of the thrice repeated 'sooteet' (which I cannot identify), the oriole's song is tried again, but is given up. The bird then metaphorically shrugs his shoulders, utters his own two rather silly notes of derision and ends with a single short sound of disgust."

   However, in a letter written to A.J.M. Smith on July 25, 1962, Glassco revealed the real and underlying reason for this strange and, for him, uncharacteristic composition. He wrote:

   > This being the lunatic season for poetry (*cf.* The ideograms, picture poems, etc. In *Alphabet* and *Delta*) I endorse this letter with my own effort, the fruits of a study of Max Müller's *Origins of Language*, are put forward: 1) language as the imitation of animal sounds (called the Bow-Wow theory), and 2) as the expression of immediate emotional reactions (the Pooh-pooh Theory). I embraced the former, and immediately sat down and wrote Catbird. Note the wonderfully sustained beauty of line 14: kooka prea, etc.

The poem appears on the reverse side with an arrow pointing to the word 'Tw'at' and the phrase 'influence of Layton' (Glassco Papers, McLennan Library, McGill University). Shortly afterwards, "Catbird" appeared in *Alphabet*, No. 6 (June 1963), and was dedicated to Marian Scott (1906–1993), the artist spouse of F.R. Scott (1899–1985).

4. THE CARDINAL'S DOG. The reference here is to a painting by the Master of Moulins, a French[?] painter of the end of the fifteenth and the beginning of the sixteenth centuries, whose identity has not been conclusively established. The picture with which Glassco is concerned in the poem is the *Nativity*, which is in the Musée d'Autun and which was painted for the Chancellor Nicolas Rolin (d. 1483).

5. George Bryan BRUMMELL (1778–1840). English dandy, distinguished for the style and elegance of his clothing and the affectation of his manners. Heir to a fortune which he managed to squander, he was forced to leave England for Calais in France in 1816 because of gambling debts. He died a pauper in a hospital for the mentally ill in Caen.

6. Théophile GAUTIER (1811–1872). French writer of the Romantic school, author of several popular novels and proponent of the 'art for art's sake' movement. He was a leader of the 'parnassians', and is best known, to-day, for his collection of poems, *Emaux et camées* (1852).

7. Antoine COYSEVOX (1640–1720). French sculptor who specialized in portraiture in stone, including a bust of Louis XIV. Some of his works, originally created for the palace at Versailles, can now be seen in the Louvre.

8. COUSTOU, the name of a family of three French sculptors, the work of one of whom, Nicolas (1658–1733), is in Notre-Dame de Paris and in the Louvre. The Chevaux de Marly, sculptures of rearing horses (copies in the place de la Concorde) by Guillaume (1677–1746), were copied for Marly-le-Roi, where Louis XIV had built a small chateau (destroyed during the revolution) with exquisite gardens and fountains.

9. Ambrose Gwinett BIERCE (1842–1914?). Eccentric American journalist and author of sardonic tales. A reclusive misanthrope, he disappeared in Mexico.

10. Cythera, an island off the south coast of Laconia, ancient region of the southern Peloponnesus, Greece. Legend has it that Aphrodite, the Greek goddess of love, landed on its shore after her miraculous birth when she issued from the foam of the sea.

11. *Montreal*, a book-length poem of six hundred and ninety-eight lines by John Glassco was published, in toto, in 1973 by DC Books, the little press which Louis Dudek established with Aileen Collins after the dissolution of DELTA CANADA in 1971. Excerpts had appeared earlier in YES 15 in September 1966.

12. *SQUIRE HARDMAN*, a flagellantine 'diversion' which was pseudonymously attributed to George Colman, was privately published by John Glassco in 1966 in a limited edition of fifty copies.

13. "THE OPAQUE MEDIUM" was first published in *META: Journal Des Traducteurs/Journal of Translators*, Vol. 14, No. 1 (mars/March 1969).

14. "Euterpe's Honeymoon: Notes on the Poetic Process" was first published in *Northern Journey* (1971). The text reproduced here is taken from a slightly modified version which Glassco submitted to *West Coast Review*, where it appeared in Vol. XII, No. 3 (February 1979).

15. The last line in the original (1971) published version of this essay was much more pointed. It reads: "I can think of many such honeymoons in poetry — above all in Canada, and especially in the French Canadian department; but I must not be local."
16. Originally published in *The Globe and Mail* in its "The Mermaid Inn" column series on November 12, 1977, p. 6.

Selected Bibliography

Poetry

The Deficit Made Flesh. Toronto: McClelland and Stewart, 1958.

A Point of Sky. Toronto: Oxford University Press (Canada), 1964.

The Poetry of French Canada in Translation. Edited and Introduced by John Glassco. Toronto: Oxford University Press (Canada), 1970.

Selected Poems. Toronto: Oxford University Press (Canada), 1971.

Squire Hardman. By George Colman. [pseud.] Foster: Pastime Press, 1966.

Montreal. Montreal: DC Books, 1973.

Prose

Under the Hill. By Aubrey Beardsley, completed by John Glassco. Paris: Olympia Press, 1959.

The English Governess. By Miles Underwood [pseud.] Paris: Ophelia Press, 1960. [Several subsequent and variant editions.]

English Poetry in Quebec. Proceedings of the Foster Poetry Conference October 12–14, 1963. Edited by John Glassco. Montreal: McGill University Press, 1965.

Memoirs of Montparnasse. Toronto: Oxford University Press (Canada), 1970. [2nd ed., introduced and annotated by Michael Gnarowski. Toronto: Oxford University Press (Canada), 1995.]

The Temple of Pederasty. Introduction by John Glassco. North Hollywood: Hanover House, 1970.

The Fatal Woman. Three Tales by John Glassco. Toronto: House of Anansi, 1974.

Translations

The Journal of Saint-Denys-Garneau. Toronto: McClelland and Stewart, 1962.

Complete Poems of Saint Denys Garneau. Ottawa: Oberon Press, 1975.

Lot's Wife. By Monique Bosco. Toronto: McClelland and Stewart, 1975.

Venus in Furs. Translated from the German by John Glassco. Burnaby: Blackfish Press, 1977.

Creatures of the Chase. By Jean-Yves Soucy. Toronto: McClelland and Stewart, 1979.

Fear's Folly (Les demi-civilisées). By Jean-Charles Harvey. Ottawa: Carleton University Press, 1982.

John Glassco: Selected Poems

This publication was produced using the T_EX typesetting system and set in Pandora.

Produced under the supervision of

Printed in the USA
CPSIA information can be obtained
at www.ICGtesting.com
JSHW051959150824
68134JS00057B/3443